SpringerBriefs in Computer Science

More information about this series at http://www.springer.com/series/10028

Paulo Shakarian • Abhinav Bhatnagar
Ashkan Aleali • Elham Shaabani
Ruocheng Guo

Diffusion in Social Networks

 Springer

Paulo Shakarian
School of Computing, Informatics
    and Decision Systems Engineering
Arizona State University
Tempe, AZ, USA

Ashkan Aleali
Arizona State University
Tempe, AZ, USA

Ruocheng Guo
Arizona State University
Tempe, AZ, USA

Abhinav Bhatnagar
Arizona State University
Tempe, AZ, USA

Elham Shaabani
Arizona State University
Tempe, AZ, USA

ISSN 2191-5768   ISSN 2191-5776   (electronic)
SpringerBriefs in Computer Science
ISBN 978-3-319-23104-4   ISBN 978-3-319-23105-1   (eBook)
DOI 10.1007/978-3-319-23105-1

Library of Congress Control Number: 2015947765

Springer Cham Heidelberg New York Dordrecht London
© The Author(s) 2015

Printed on acid-free paper

Springer International Publishing AG Switzerland is part of Springer Science+Business Media (www.springer.com)

Preface

In recent years, research on diffusion process in social networks has grown in a variety of fields including computer science, physics, and biology. However, often times research in these individual disciplines becomes stove-piped. In this book, we focus on cutting-edge research in social network diffusion bringing together a range of ideas from these disciplines with the goal of creating a single volume that examines these ideas.

We sought to cover many of the most important concepts, models, and methods from these areas. We felt by exploring a variety of work from different fields that we could help open the door to more innovative findings in this fascinating area of diffusion in social networks.

Tempe, AZ, USA
May 2015

Paulo Shakarian
Abhinav Bhatnagar
Ashkan Aleali
Elham Shaabani
Ruocheng Guo

Acknowledgements

The authors would like to acknowledge the generous support from Arizona State University, the Army Research Office, the Air Force Office of Scientific Research, and the Office of Naval Research that have enabled our research in the area of social network diffusion. We would also like to thank the following collaborators who have contributed to some of the research that is reviewed in this volume: Anthony Johnson, Brian Macdonald, Christian Molinaro, Damon Paulo, Geoffrey Moores, Gerardo Simari, Hansheng Lei, Luke Gerdes, Matthias Broecheler, Nicholas Howard, Patrick Roos, Maria Luisa Sapino, Sean Eyre, and V.S. Subrhamanian.

Acknowledgeents

Contents

Chapter 1
Introduction

This book introduces the readers to recent research concerning diffusion in social networks and attempts bring together disparate lines of work on the topic from multiple fields. The availability of large social network datasets over nearly the past two decades have made it possible to explore network diffusion like never before. Having said that, the materials covered in this book is not limited to the online platforms, but rather are thought to be applicable to social networks from a variety of domains. Similar to other subjects in social network analysis, information diffusion has its roots in multiple field of study: biologists and physicists have done research in the field by studying evolutionary dynamics [2] and disease propagation models [3]; economist and Nobel Laureate Thomas Schelling introduced the idea of "tipping points" which now has become mainstream [4]; concurrently Mark Granovetter studied these ideas from a sociological perspective [5]. However, it wasn't until Kempe et al. article [1] in 2003 that information diffusion became a significant line of research in computer science.

In this volume, we look to provide an overview of the major diffusion models seen in multiple disciplines. First we examine the popular SIR model—which has been studied in biology and physics. This is followed by a chapter on the "tipping" model—which has its roots in economics and sociology and is prevalent in mathematics and some computer science venues. We then turn our attention to the independent cascade and linear threshold models that are often explored in data mining. Then we discuss the artificial intelligence community's logic programming based diffusion models. After that, we examine models based on evolutionary dynamics such as the voter model—which have become popular with theoretical biologists and the statistical physics community. Finally, we briefly examine some work related to observing and reasoning about diffusion processes in the real world.

To sum up, research in social network analysis in general, and information diffusion in social networks in particular is still in its early stages. We try to give a good overview of the work done so far. We hope that the reader finds the material useful and a good starting point for cutting-edge research in this area.

© The Author(s) 2015
P. Shakarian et al., *Diffusion in Social Networks*, SpringerBriefs
in Computer Science, DOI 10.1007/978-3-319-23105-1_1

References

1. Kempe, David, Jon Kleinberg, and Éva Tardos. "Maximizing the spread of influence through a social network." Proceedings of the ninth ACM SIGKDD international conference on Knowledge discovery and data mining. ACM, 2003.
2. Moran, P., 1958. Random processes in genetics. Mathematical Proceedings of the Cambridge Philosophical Society 54 (01), 60–71.
3. Anderson, Roy M., May, Robert M. (1979). Population biology of infectious diseases: Part i. 280 (5721), 361.
4. Schelling, T.C. (1978). Micromotives and Macrobehavior. W.W. Norton and Co.
5. Granovetter, M. (1978). Threshold models of collective behavior. The American Journal of Sociology (6), 1420–1443.

Chapter 2
The SIR Model and Identification of Spreaders

2.1 Introduction

In this chapter, we study one of the most ubiquitous diffusion models: the susceptible-infected-recovered (SIR) model. Considering a network structure, a key problem relating to SIR model is how to identify the nodes that, if initially infected, will result in the greatest expected infected population. These nodes are often referred to as "spreaders". Unfortunately, exactly computing the expected number of infected individuals in a network-structured population given a single initial infectee is #P-hard (we shall discuss this complexity result further in Chap. 4). This implies that solving this problem exactly is likely beyond the ability of today's computer systems. However, the literature on complex networks has provided various nodal measures that can be used as heuristics. In this chapter, we review various nodal measures and examine the utility of these measures as heuristics to find spreaders under the SIR model. These experiments show that the ability of nodal measures to identify spreaders in the SIR Model.

With these experiments, we carefully selected the parameter β based on β', the *epidemic threshold* of the network. We can be sure that a contagion can spread to a significant portion of the network for $\beta > \beta'$, and we studied a variety of different values for β above this threshold.

The rest of this chapter is organized as follows. In Sect. 2.2, we review the SIR model and describe how we calculate the epidemic threshold of a given complex network. This is followed by a review of the various centrality and other nodal measures we will study in Sect. 2.3 along with a recap of the description of the "imprecision function" [17] used to measure the effectiveness of a nodal measure in identifying the top spreaders in a network. We give a description and discussion of the experimental results in Sect. 2.4.

© The Author(s) 2015
P. Shakarian et al., *Diffusion in Social Networks*, SpringerBriefs
in Computer Science, DOI 10.1007/978-3-319-23105-1_2

2.2   The SIR Model

As in [17], we consider the classic susceptible-infected-recovered (SIR) model of disease spread introduced in [2]. In this model, all nodes in the network are in one of three states: susceptible (able to be infected), infected, or recovered (no longer able to infect or be infected). At each time step, only node infected in the last time step can infect any of its neighbors who are in a susceptible state with a probability β. After that time step, the node previously in an infected state moves into a recovered state and is no longer able to infect or be infected.

2.2.1   Selecting the Infection Probability

We note that for scale-free networks, having degree distribution $P(k) \sim k^{-\gamma}$, the literature shows that for $\gamma \leq 3$, the epidemic threshold of β approaches 0 as the number of nodes goes to infinity [10, 14]. However, the networks we examine are of finite size and have various levels of "scale-freeness", based on the R^2 value of the linear correlation of a log-log plot of the degree distribution (see Sect. 2.4.1 for details). Instead, we explored β values based on the epidemic threshold calculation in [20]. Using this method, the SIR model is mapped onto a bond percolation process. Assuming a randomly connected network, the average number of influenced neighbors, $\langle n \rangle$ can be written

$$\langle n \rangle = \beta \cdot \sum_k \frac{P(k) \cdot k \cdot (k-1)}{\langle k \rangle}, \tag{2.1}$$

where k is the degree of a node, $P(k)$ is the probability of a node having degree k, and $\langle k \rangle$ is the average degree. Since an epidemic state can only be reached when $\langle n \rangle > 1$, and from (2.1) we have

$$\beta > \left(\sum_k \frac{P(k) \cdot k \cdot (k-1)}{\langle k \rangle} \right)^{-1} = \beta'. \tag{2.2}$$

We note that there is some work discussing the effect of different infection probabilities on spreading in [17] and more recent and comprehensive study on the topic in [12]. These works consider the effect of this parameter with respect to degree and shell decomposition (and betweenness in [17]). Here we consider these and many other nodal measures, and find that some of them, such as eigenvector centrality, outperform those in these previous works.

2.3 Centrality and Other Nodal Measures

We now describe the centrality measures that we examine in our experiments. We note that the major centrality measures in the literature can be classified as either radial (the quantity of certain paths originating from the node) or medial (the quantity of certain paths passing through the node) as done in Borgatti and Everett [6]. Based on the negative result concerning betweenness of Kitsak et al. [17] and the intuitive association between high-radial nodes and spreading, we focused our efforts on radial measures. While the work of Kitsak et al. [17] compares shell number to degree and betweenness, we consider several other well-known radial measures in addition to degree, including closeness and eigenvector centrality. As done in [17], we also develop "imprecision functions" for these centrality measures.

2.3.1 Degree Centrality

Of all the measures that we are examining, degree is perhaps the most simplistic measure—simply the total of incident edges for a given node. As noted throughout the literature, such as [24], it is perhaps the easiest centrality measure to compute. Further, in other diffusion processes, such as the voter model on undirected networks in [1], it has been shown to be proportional to the expected number of individuals becoming infected[1] (we discuss these results in detail in Chap. 6). As pointed out in [6], degree is a radial measure as it is the number of paths starting from a node of length 1. Degree is one of three measures considered in [17].

2.3.2 Shell Number

The other radial measure considered in [17], shell number, or "k-shell number", is determined using shell decomposition [23]. High shell-number nodes in the network are often referred to as the "core" and are regarded by Kitsak et al. [17] as influential spreaders under the SIR model. Our results described later in this chapter confirm this finding, although we also show that shell number was generally outperformed by eigenvector centrality. There have also been some more practical applications of this technique to find key nodes in a network. For instance, Borge-Holthoefer and Moreno [7, 8] uses shell-decomposition to find individuals likely to initiate

---

[1]Technically, the work of Antal et al. [1] proves that the fixation probability for a single mutant invader is proportional to the degree of that node. However, the expected number of mutants, in the limit as time goes to infinity, can simply be computed by multiplying fixation probability by the number of nodes in the network.

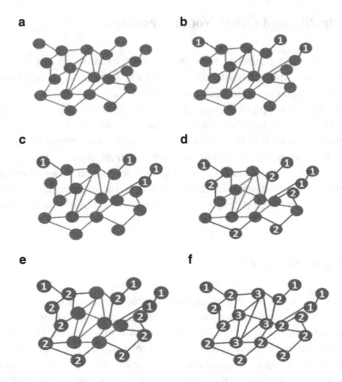

Fig. 2.1 Consider the progression of the graph above, where the elimination of nodes with degree 1 occurs in B and C. D represents the first iteration for the second shell, and E represents the complete second shell (as well as the first). F finalizes the decomposition with the third shell

information cascades in an online social network while [11] uses it to identify key nodes in a subset of autonomous systems on the Internet.

An example of this process is shown in Fig. 2.1. Given graph $G = (V, E)$, shell decomposition partitions a graph into shells and is described in the algorithm below.

Let k_i be the degree of node i. Set $S = 1$. Let V_S denote the first shell of G.
while $|V| > 0$ **do**
    while There exists i such that $k_i = S$ **do**
        Remove all $i \in V$ where $k_i = S$;
        Also, remove all corresponding adjacent edges.
        Place removed nodes into shell V_S.
    end while
    S++
end while

2.3.3 Betweenness Centrality

The intuition behind high betweenness centrality nodes is that they function as "bottlenecks" as many paths in the network pass through them. Hence, betweenness is a medial centrality measure. Let σ_{st} be the number of shortest paths between nodes s and t and $\sigma_{st}(v)$ be the number of shortest paths between s and t containing node v. In [15], betweenness centrality for node v is defined as $\sum_{s \neq v \neq t} \frac{\sigma_{st}(v)}{\sigma_{st}}$. In most implementations, including the ones used in this chapter, the algorithm of Brandes [9] is used to calculate betweenness centrality.

2.3.4 Closeness Centrality

Another common measure from the literature that we examined is closeness [16]. Given node i, its closeness $C_c(i)$ is the inverse of the average shortest path length from node i to all other nodes in the graph. Intuitively, closeness measures how "close" it is to all other nodes in a graph.

Formally, if we define the shortest path between nodes i to j as function $d_G(i,j)$, we can express the average path length from i to all other nodes as

$$L_i = \frac{\sum_{j \in V \setminus i} d_G(i,j)}{|V| - 1}. \tag{2.3}$$

Hence, the closeness of a node can be formally written as

$$C_c(i) = \frac{1}{L_i} = \frac{|V| - 1}{\sum_{j \in V \setminus i} d_G(i,j)}. \tag{2.4}$$

2.3.5 Eigenvector Centrality

The use of the principle eigenvector of the adjacency matrix of a network was first proposed as a centrality measure in [5]. Hence, the intuition behind eigenvector centrality is that it measures the influence of a node based on the sum of the influences of its adjacent nodes. Given a network $V = (G,E)$ with adjacency matrix $A = (a_{ij})$, where $a_{ij} = 1$ if an edge exists between nodes i and j, the eigenvector centrality of node i satisfies

$$x_i = \frac{1}{\lambda} \sum_{j \in V} a_{ij} x_j, \tag{2.5}$$

for some λ. If we define x to be the vector of x_i's, this relationship can be expressed as

$$x = \frac{1}{\lambda}Ax, \text{ or } Ax = \lambda x, \tag{2.6}$$

which is the familiar equation relating A with its eigenvalues and eigenvector. The eigenvector centralities for the network are the entries of the eigenvector corresponding to the largest real eigenvalue.

2.3.6 PageRank

PageRank, introduced in [22], is computed for each node based on the PageRank of its neighbors. Where E is the set of undirected edges, R_v, d_v is the PageRank and degree of v, and c is a normalization constant, we have the relationship

$$R_v = c \cdot \sum_{v'|(v,v')\in E} \frac{R_{v'}}{d_{v'}}.$$

An initial value for rank is entered for each node and the relationship is then computed iteratively until convergence is reached. Intuitively, PageRank can be thought of as the importance of a node based on the importance of its neighbors.

2.3.7 Neighborhood

The next nodal measure we consider is the "neighborhood." Given a natural number q, the q-neighborhood of vertex i is the number of nodes in the network that are distance q or closer from node i. For example, for $q = 0$, this metric is 1 for every node. For $q = 1$, this metric is identical to degree centrality of node i, since it is the number of nodes within a distance 1 of i. For $q = 2$, this metric counts the number of nodes within a distance 2 of i, so it counts i's neighbors along with its neighbors' neighbors. In our work, we computed neighborhoods using $q = 2,3,5,10$, and denoted these measures by $nghd2$, $nghd3$, $nghd5$, and $nghd10$, respectively. We note that the work of Chen et al. [13] develops a centrality measure with a similar intuition to the neighborhood and show it performs well in identifying influential spreaders.

2.3.8 The Imprecision Functions

We now define the imprecision functions from [17] that are used to measure the effectiveness of a nodal measure in identifying influential spreaders. We also extend their definition for all nodal measures explored in this chapter. Let N denote the number of nodes, and let p be a real number between 0 and 100. The $pN/100$ highest efficiency spreaders, $\Upsilon_{eff}(p)$, are chosen based on number of nodes infected M_i per node. Similarly, a set $\Upsilon_{k_s}(p)$ is defined as the $pN/100$ predicted most efficient spreaders, chosen with priority to highest k_s valued nodes. Let

$$M_{eff}(p) = \sum_{i \in \Upsilon_{eff}(p)} \frac{M_i}{pN}, and \tag{2.7}$$

$$M_{k_s}(p) = \sum_{i \in \Upsilon_{k_s}(p)} \frac{M_i}{pN}. \tag{2.8}$$

The imprecision function of k_s, $\varepsilon_{k_s}(p)$, is defined as

$$\varepsilon_{k_s}(p) = 1 - \frac{M_{k_s}(p)}{M_{eff}(p)} \tag{2.9}$$

Similarly, $\varepsilon_{eig}(p)$ and $\varepsilon_{deg}(p)$ are defined as

$$\varepsilon_{eig}(p) = 1 - \frac{M_{eig}(p)}{M_{eff}(p)}, \tag{2.10}$$

$$\varepsilon_{deg}(p) = 1 - \frac{M_{deg}(p)}{M_{eff}(p)} \tag{2.11}$$

In general, for any nodal measure c, the imprecision function $\varepsilon_c(p)$ is defined as

$$\varepsilon_c(p) = 1 - \frac{M_c(p)}{M_{eff}(p)} \tag{2.12}$$

2.4 Experimental Findings

In this section, we will briefly recap some of our previous experiments involving the identification of spreaders under the SIR model using nodal measures. Please refer to [3] for the complete technical report.

2.4.1 Datasets

We obtained our datasets from a variety of sources. Brief descriptions of these networks are as follows:

cond-mat-GCC is an academic collaboration network from the e-print arXiv and covers scientific collaborations between authors' papers submitted to Condensed Matter category from 1999 [21].

ca-GrQc-GCC is an academic collaboration network from the e-print arXiv and covers scientific collaborations between authors' papers submitted to the General Relativity and Quantum Cosmology category from Jan. 1993 to Apr. 2003 [18].

urv-email is an e-mail network based on communications of members of the University Rovira i Virgili (Tarragona) [4]. It was extracted in 2003.

1-edges-GCC is a network formed from YouTube, the video-sharing website that allows users to establish friendship links [25]. The sample was extracted in Dec. 2008. Links represent two individuals sharing one or more subscriptions to channels on YouTube.

std-GCC is an online sex community in Brazil in which links represent that one of the individuals posted online about a sexual experience with the other individual, resulting in a bipartite graph. The data was extracted from September of 2002 to October of 2008 [19].

as20000102 is a one day snapshot of Internet routers as constructed from the border gateway protocol logs [18]. It was extracted on Jan 2nd, 2000.

oregon_010331 is a network of Internet routers over a one week period as inferred from Oregon route-views, looking glass data, and routing registry from covering the week of March 3rd, 2001 [18].

ca-HepTh-GCC is a collaboration network from the e-print arXiv and covers scientific collaborations between authors' papers submitted to the High Energy Physics—Theory category. It covers paper from Jan 1993 to Apr 2003 [18].

as-22July06 is a snapshot of the Internet on 22 July 2006 at the autonomous systems level compiled by Mark Newman [21].

netscience-GCC is a network of coauthorship of scientists working on network theory and experiments compiled by Mark Newman in May 2006 [21].

All datasets used for this chapter were obtained from one of four sources: the ASU Social Computing Data Repository [25], the Stanford Network Analysis Project [18], Mark Newman's data repository at the University of Michigan [21], and Universitat Rovira i Virgili [4]. All networks considered were symmetric; i.e., if a directed edge from vertex v to v' exists, there is also an edge from vertex v' to v. Summary statistics for these networks can be found in Table 2.1.

In the cases where the network had more than one connected component, we used only the greatest one. We append the suffix "-GCC" when referring to those networks. For example, the cond-mat network had more than one component, so we will use the greatest connected component and refer to this network as "cond-mat-GCC".

Table 2.1 Network summary statistics

Name	Type	Nodes	Edges	Density	β'	λ	R^2	$\langle k \rangle$	$\langle k^2 \rangle$	K_S
1-edges-GCC	Online	13679	76741	0.0008	2.3	1.8	0.90	11.2	502.6	25
as20000102	Router	6474	12572	0.0006	0.6	1.2	0.73	3.9	640.0	12
ca-GrQc-GCC	Collab	4158	13422	0.0016	6.3	2.0	0.88	5.5	93.2	43
cond-mat-GCC	Collab	13861	44619	0.0005	8.4	2.4	0.93	5.9	75.6	17
oregon2_010331	Router	10900	31180	0.0005	0.5	1.2	0.79	5.7	1188.8	31
std-GCC	Std	15810	38540	0.0003	3.7	1.9	0.92	4.7	130.9	11
urv-email	Email	1133	5451	0.0085	5.7	1.5	0.84	9.6	179.8	11
ca-HepTh-GCC	Collab	8638	24806	0.0007	8.3	2.2	0.90	5.7	74.6	31
as-22July2006	Router	22963	48436	0.0002	0.4	1.2	0.72	4.2	1103.0	25
netscience-GCC	Collab	379	914	0.0127	14.2	1.6	0.76	4.8	38.7	8

Note that β' is the minimum threshold of infection rate for the epidemic to spread to a significant portion of the network, λ is exponent of the power law of the degree distribution, R^2 is goodness of fit between the power law and the degree distribution, $\langle k \rangle$ and $\langle k^2 \rangle$ are the first and second moments of the degree distribution, and K_S is the maximum shell present in the network

Fig. 2.2 In the higher shells of these two examples, degree and shell number are not correlated, indicating these can not be assumed to be generated by preferential attachment models. The *red line* shows the average degree of each shell. Note that log scales are being used on both axes

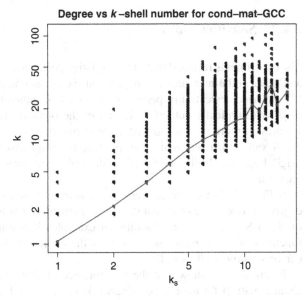

As seen in the Table 2.1, all networks used are approximately scale free. This does not infer that they were generated using a preferential attachment model, as many mechanisms can be responsible for generating scale free networks. If they were generated using a preferential attachment model then we would see a correlation between shell number and degree. This would also mean that degree centrality and shell number would have little difference in predicting spreaders, but our simulations show otherwise. Figure 2.2 shows an example in which degree and shell number are not correlated.

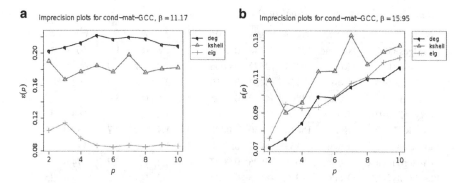

Fig. 2.3 Imprecision plots vs. p for the cond-mat network with different β. (**a**) Imprecision versus p for the cond-mat network with $\beta = 11.17$. Notice that for this β, k-shell has a lower imprecision, meaning that shell number outperforms degree. See Sect. 2.3 for the definitions of imprecision function and p. (**b**) Imprecision plots vs. p for the cond-mat network with $\beta = 15.95$. Notice that for this β, degree has a lower imprecision, meaning that degree outperforms shell number, the opposite of what we saw in Fig. 2.3a

2.4.2 Sensitivity to β

The experiments revealed that (1) the relative performance of degree, shell number and other nodal measures can depend on the β parameter of the SIR model, and (2) eigenvector centrality performs very well in general regardless of the value of β used, typically outperforming all of the other measures that we tried. Here we present more results illustrating these two points. Unless otherwise specified, the β values that we used when plotting the imprecision function versus β are $1.1\beta', 1.2\beta', \ldots, 2.0\beta'$, where β' is the epidemic threshold for the network in question.

In Fig. 2.3a, b, we give an example of a network where shell number outperforms degree for one value of β, but degree outperforms shell number for another value of β. In Sect. 2.4, we give additional examples illustrating that the imprecision functions of other measures, as well as the choice of the "best" nodal measure, can be sensitive to β as well.

Figure 2.3a, b show that the performance of degree relative to shell number changes with β for the cond-mat network. For $\beta = 11.17$, shell number is a better indicator of spreading, but for $\beta = 15.95$, degree is better. Another way that we could depict this dependence on β is to fix p and plot the imprecision versus β, instead of fixing β and plotting the imprecision versus p. In Fig. 2.4a, we fix $p = 5$ and plot the imprecision function of degree, shell number, and eigenvector centrality versus β, for β between 11.17 and 15.95. As it shows, degree outperforms shell number after β gets large enough.

The relative performance of other centrality measures can change as well. In Fig. 2.4b, we plot the imprecision functions of degree, shell number, eigenvector, and closeness centrality versus β for $p = 5$.

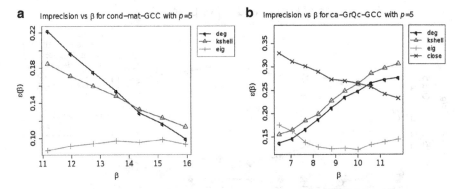

Fig. 2.4 Imprecision vs. β for the cond-mat network and ca-GrQc-GCC network. (**a**) Imprecision vs. β for the cond-mat network. The relative performance of degree and shell number changes near $\beta = 14$. (**b**) Imprecision vs. β for the ca-GrQc-GCC network

In this network, for β near β', degree and shell number perform very well. However, as β increases, the imprecision functions of those measures increase, and other measures, like closeness and eigenvector, outperform degree and shell number.

2.4.3 Eigenvector Centrality for Spreader Identification

The experiments show that eigenvector centrality consistently outperforms all other measures considered, including both shell number and degree (which were considered by Kitsak et al.), in all but one of the networks examined. See Fig. 2.5 for a comparison of shell number (the best performing measure of Kitsak et al.) with eigenvector centrality. Also, if we average over all of our networks, including the one where eigenvector was not the best, we find that, on average, eigenvector centrality outperforms the other measures.

As we saw in Fig. 2.5, eigenvector centrality outperforms shell number for all but one of the networks we examined. Eigenvector centrality also typically outperforms all of the other measures that we tried. In Fig. 2.6a, we plot the imprecision functions of several different measures for the cond-mat network. We see that eigenvector centrality performs best for this network. In Figs. 2.6b and 2.7a–c, we give examples of a collaboration network, an online network, a STD network and an email network in which eigenvector performs best.

Eigenvector centrality does not outperform shell number for the ca-HepTh network, so we can not conclude that eigenvector centrality performs best for *every* network that we tried. However, it does seem that, *on average*, for the networks we considered, eigenvector centrality performs best for $\beta = 1.1\beta', 1.2\beta', \ldots, 2.0\beta'$. Suppose we take the imprecision functions for $\beta = 1.1\beta'$ for each network, and we average these imprecision functions over all of our networks, including the

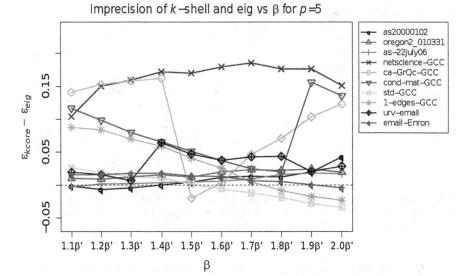

Fig. 2.5 Imprecision of k-shell minus the imprecision of eigenvector centrality. Positive values indicate that shell number has a higher imprecision than eigenvector centrality, which means that eigenvector centrality typically outperforms shell number

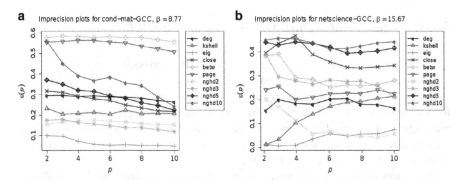

Fig. 2.6 Imprecision vs. p for the cond-mat-GCC network and netscience-GCC network. (a) Imprecision vs. p for the cond-mat-GCC network with $\beta = 1.1\beta' = 8.77$. We see that eigenvalue centrality performs best for this network. (b) Imprecision vs. p for the netscience-GCC network with $\beta = 1.1\beta' = 15.67$. We see that eigenvalue centrality performs best for this network

ca-HepTh network. This would be one way to check how well each measure performs on average. In Fig. 2.8, we plot this the average imprecision versus p for $\beta = 1.1\beta'$. We see that, on average, eigenvector centrality outperforms the other measures. The measure *nghd2* performs well also. We show similar results for $\beta = 1.5\beta'$ and $\beta = 2.0\beta'$ in Fig. 2.9a, b. In both cases, eigenvector centrality outperforms all of the other measures.

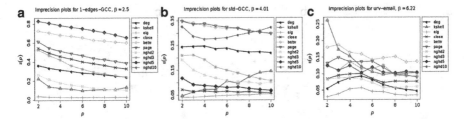

Fig. 2.7 Imprecision vs. p for 1-edges-GCC, std-GCC and urv-email network. (**a**) Imprecision vs. p for the 1-edges-GCC network with $\beta = 1.1\beta' = 2.50$. We see that eigenvalue centrality performs best for this network. (**b**) Imprecision vs. p for the std-GCC network with $\beta = 1.1\beta' = 4.01$. We see that eigenvalue centrality performs best for this network. (**c**) Imprecision vs. p for the urv-email network with $\beta = 1.1\beta' = 6.22$. We see that eigenvalue centrality performs best for this network

Fig. 2.8 Average imprecision vs. p with $\beta = 1.1\beta'$, where the average is taken over all networks that we considered

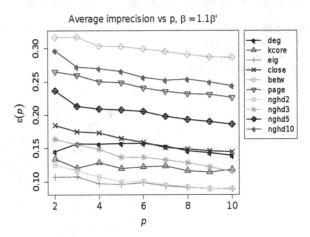

We believe that eigenvector centrality performs well for some of the same reasons that shell number performs well. A node has high eigenvector centrality when the node and its neighbors have high degree. Nghd2, nghd3, and the closely related measure of Chen et al. [13] also perform well for this reason. A hub, or a node with high degree, in the periphery of a network, which does not have many neighbors with high degree, will not typically be as good of a spreader as a node with high eigenvector centrality.

2.4.4 Large Values of β

In [17], only relatively small values for β were explored as it was noted that larger values of β would likely cause spreading to a large portion of the population regardless of the location of the initially infected node. However, in the networks we studied, we found a difference in the ability of the starting node to spread even

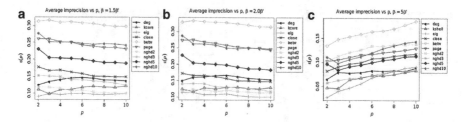

Fig. 2.9 Average imprecision vs. p with different β. (**a**) Average imprecision vs. p with $\beta = 1.5\beta'$, where the average is taken over all networks that we considered. We see that, on average, eigenvector performs best. (**b**) Average imprecision vs. p with $\beta = 2.0\beta'$, where the average is taken over all networks that we considered. We see that, on average, eigenvector performs best. (**c**) Average imprecision vs. p with $\beta = 5\beta'$, where the average is taken over all networks that we considered. We see that, on average, eigenvector performs best

Fig. 2.10 Average imprecision vs. β with $p = 5$. We see that, on average, eigenvector performs best

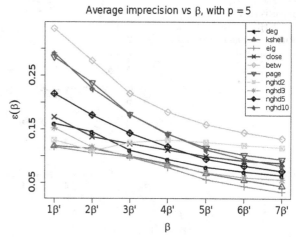

at seven times the epidemic threshold. Further, the result that eigenvector centrality performs best, based on average imprecision over all the networks, still holds for these large values of β. We display our imprecision functions for large values of β in Fig. 2.10. We also show that for five times the epidemic threshold, eigenvector centrality still outperforms the other centrality measures for different values of p (Fig. 2.9c).

2.5 Conclusions

In this chapter we studied the SIR model and looked at identifying nodes that cause diffusion to spread to a large extent based on various nodal measures. However, we made two assumptions—that the infection probability was the same amongst all edges and that we only looked for single "spreaders". In the Chap. 4, we make efforts to find *sets* of nodes and extend the model to allow for different infection probabilities amongst the edges.

References

1. Antal, T., Redner, S., Sood, V. (2006). Evolutionary dynamics on degree-heterogeneous graphs. Physical review letters, 96 (18), 188104.
2. Anderson, Roy M., May, Robert M. (1979). Population biology of infectious diseases: Part i. 280 (5721), 361.
3. Macdonald, B., Shakarian, P., Howard, N., Moores, G. (2012). Spreaders in the Network SIR Model: An Empirical Study. (USMA Technical Report).
4. Arenas, Alex. (2012). Network data sets.
5. Bonacich, Phillip. (1972). Factoring and weighting approaches to status scores and clique identification. The journal of mathematical sociology. 2 (1), 113–120.
6. Borgatti, S., Everett, M. (2006). A Graph-theoretic perspective on centrality. Social networks 28 (4), 466–484.
7. Borge-Holthoefer, Javier, & Moreno, Yamir. (2012). Absence of influential spreaders in rumor dynamics. Phys. rev. e, 85 (026116).
8. Borge-Holthoefer, Javier, Rivero, Alejandro, & Moreno, Yamir. (2012). Locating privileged spreaders on an online social network. Phys. rev. e 85 (Jun), 066123.
9. Brandes, Ulrik. (2001). A faster algorithm for betweenness centrality. Journal of mathematical sociology, 25 (163).
10. Callaway, Duncan S., Newman, M. E. J., Strogatz, Steven H., & Watts, Duncan J. (2000). Network robustness and fragility: Percolation on random graphs. Phys. rev. lett. , 85(Dec), 5468–5471.
11. Carmi, Shai, Havlin, Shlomo, Kirkpatrick, Scott, Shavitt, Yuval, & Shir, Eran (2007). From the Cover: A model of Internet topology using k-shell decomposition. Pnas , 104 (27), 11150–11154.
12. Castellano, & Pastor-Satorras, Romualdo. (2012). Competing activation mechanisms in epidemics on networks. Scientific reports, 2 (371).
13. Chen, Duanbing, L, Linyuan, Shang, Ming-Sheng, Zhang, Yi-Cheng, & Zhou, Tao (2012). Identifying influential nodes in complex networks. Physics a: Statistical mechanics and its applications, 391(4), 1777–1787.
14. Cohen, Reuven, Erez, Keren, ben Avraham, Daniel, & Havlin, Shlomo. (2000). Resilience of the Internet to Random Breakdowns. Physical review letters, 85(21), 4626–4628.
15. Freeman, Linton C. (1977). A set of measures of centrality based on betweenness. Sociometry, 40(1), pp. 35–41.
16. Freeman, Linton C. (1979). Centrality in social networks conceptual clarification. Social networks, 1 (3), 215–239.
17. Kitsak, Maksim, Gallos, Lazaros K., Havlin, Shlomo, Liljeros, Fredrik, Muchnik, Lev, Stanley, H. Eugene, & Makse, Hernan A. (2010). Identification of influential spreaders in complex networks. Nat phys, 6 (11), 888–893.
18. Leskovec, Jure. (2012). Stanford network analysis project (snap).
19. Luis E. C. Rocha, Fredrik Liljeros, & Holme, Petter. (2010). Information dynamics shape the sexual networks of internet-mediated prostitution. Proceedings of the national academy of sciences, March.
20. Madar, N., Kalisky, T., Cohen, R., ben Avraham, D., & Havlin, S. (2004). Immunization and epidemic dynamics in complex networks.The European physical journal b - condensed matter and complex systems, 38 (2), 269–276.

21. Newman, Mark. (2011). Network data.
22. Page, L., Brin, S., Motwani, R., & Winograd, T. (1998). The pagerank citation ranking: Bringing order to the web. Pages 161–172 of: Proceedings of the 7th international world wide web conference.
23. Seidman, Stephen B. (1983). Network structure and minimum degree. Social networks, 5 (3), 269–287.
24. Wasserman, Stanley, & Faust, Katherine. (1994). Social network analysis: Methods and applications. 1 edn. Structural analysis in the social sciences, no. 8. Cambridge University Press.
25. Zafarani, R., & Liu, H. (2009). Social computing data repository at ASU.

Chapter 3
The Tipping Model and the Minimum Seed Problem

3.1 Introduction

A much studied model in the context of social network diffusion, tipping [9, 10, 17] (a.k.a. deterministic linear threshold [11]) is often associated with "seed" or "target" set selection, [7] (a.k.a. the maximum influence problem). Tipping models first became popular by the works of Granovetter [9] and Schelling [17] where it was presented primarily in a social context. Since then, several variants have been introduced in the literature including the non-deterministic version of [11] (described later in Chap. 4) and a generalized version of [10] (discussed in Chap. 5). In this chapter, we focus on the deterministic version. In [19], the authors look at deterministic tipping where each node is activated upon a percentage of neighbors being activated. Dryer and Roberts [8] introduce the MIN-SEED problem (sometimes referred to as target set selection), study its complexity, and describe several of its properties w.r.t. certain special cases of graphs/networks. The hardness of approximation for this problem is described in [7]. The work of Ben-Zwi et al. [3] presents an algorithm for target-set selection whose complexity is determined by the tree-width of the graph. The work of Reichman [16] proves a non-trivial upper bound on the smallest seed set.

In target set selection problem (a.k.a. seed set selection), we have a social network in the form of a directed graph and a threshold for each individual. Based on this data, the desired output is the smallest possible set of individuals (seed set) such that, if initially activated, the entire population will become activated (adopting the new property). When a cardinality constraint is imposed, this problem is NP-Complete [8, 11] so approximation algorithms must be used. Though some such algorithms have been proposed, [3, 7, 14] none of them can be scaled to very large data sets. In this chapter, we use the intuition of shell decomposition, [2, 5, 12] we present a method guaranteed to find a set of nodes that causes the entire population to activate—but is not necessarily of minimal size. We then evaluate the algorithm on 31 large, real-world, social networks and show that it often finds very small

© The Author(s) 2015
P. Shakarian et al., *Diffusion in Social Networks*, SpringerBriefs
in Computer Science, DOI 10.1007/978-3-319-23105-1_3

seed sets (often several orders of magnitude smaller than the population size). We also show that the size of a seed set is related to Louvain modularity and average clustering coefficient. Therefore, we find that dense community structure combined with tight-knit local neighborhoods inhibit the spreading of activation under the tipping model. We also found that our algorithm outperforms the classic centrality measures (such as those discussed in Chap. 2) and is robust against the removal of high-degree nodes.

The rest of the chapter is organized as follows. In Sect. 3.2, we provide formal definitions of the tipping model. This is followed by the presentation of algorithms in Sect. 3.3. We then describe the experimental results in Sect. 3.4.

3.2 The Tipping Model

Throughout this chapter we assume the existence of a *social network,* $G = (V, E)$, where V is a set of vertices and E is a set of directed edges. We will use the notation n and m for the cardinality of V and E respectively. For a given node $v_i \in V$, the set of incoming neighbors is η_i^{in}, and the set of outgoing neighbors is η_i^{out}. The cardinalities of these sets (and hence the in- and out-degrees of node v_i) are d_i^{in}, d_i^{out} respectively. We now define a threshold function that for each node returns the fraction of incoming neighbors that must be activated for it to become activate as well.

Definition 3.1 (Threshold Function). We define the **threshold function** as mapping from V to $(0, 1]$. Formally: $\theta : V \to (0, 1]$.

For the number of neighbors that must be active, we will use the shorthand k_i. Hence, for each v_i, $k_i = \lceil \theta(v_i) \cdot d_i^{in} \rceil$. We now define an *activation function* that, given an initial set of active nodes, returns a set of active nodes after one time step.

Definition 3.2 (Activation Function). Given a threshold function, θ, an **activation function** A_θ maps subsets of V to subsets of V, where for some $V' \subseteq V$,

$$A_\theta(V') = V' \cup \{v_i \in V \ s.t. \ |\eta_i^{in} \cap V'| \geq k_i\} \tag{3.1}$$

We now define multiple applications of the activation function.

Definition 3.3 (Multiple Applications of the Activation Function). Given a natural number $i > 0$, set $V' \subseteq V$, and threshold function, θ, we define the multiple applications of the activation function, $A_\theta^i(V')$, as follows:

$$A_\theta^i(V') = \begin{cases} A_\theta(V') & \text{if } i = 1 \\ A_\theta(A_\theta^{i-1}(V')) & \text{otherwise} \end{cases} \tag{3.2}$$

Clearly, when $A_\theta^i(V') = A_\theta^{i-1}(V')$ the process has converged. Further, this always converges in no more than n steps (as, prior to converging, a process must, in each step, activate at least one new node). Based on this idea, we define the function Γ which returns the set of all nodes activated upon the convergence of the activation function.

Definition 3.4 (Γ Function). Let j be the least value such that $A_\theta^j(V') = A_\theta^{j-1}(V')$. We define the function $\Gamma_\theta : 2^V \to 2^V$ as follows.

$$\Gamma_\theta(V') = A_\theta^j(V') \tag{3.3}$$

3.3 The Minimum Seed Problem

We now have all the pieces to introduce our problem—finding the minimal number of nodes that are initially active to ensure that the entire set V becomes active.

Definition 3.5 (The MIN-SEED Problem). The MIN-SEED Problem is defined as follows: given a threshold function, θ, return $V' \subseteq V$ s.t. $\Gamma_\theta(V') = V$, and there does not exist $V'' \subseteq V$ where $|V''| < |V'|$ and $\Gamma_\theta(V'') = V$.

The following theorem is from the literature [8, 11] and tells us that the MIN-SEED problem is NP-complete.

Theorem 3.1 (Complexity of MIN-SEED [8, 11]). *MIN-SEED in NP-Complete.*

Now, we introduce an integer program that solved the MIN-SEED problem exactly and our new decomposition-based heuristic.

3.3.1 Exact Approach

Below we present SEED-IP, an integer program that if solved exactly, guarantees an exact solution to MIN-SEED (see Proposition 3.1). Though, in general, solving an integer program is also NP-hard, suggesting that an exact solution will likely take exponential time, good approximation techniques such as branch-and-bound exist and mature tools such as QSopt and CPLEX can readily take and approximate solutions to integer programs.

Definition 3.6 (SEED-IP).

$$\min \textstyle\sum_i x_{i,1}, \quad w.r.t. \tag{3.4}$$

$$\forall i, t \in \{1, \ldots, n\}, \quad x_{i,t} \in \{0, 1\} \tag{3.5}$$

$$\forall i, \quad x_{i,n} = 1 \tag{3.6}$$

$$\forall i, \forall t > 0, \quad x_{i,t} \leq x_{i,t-1} + \frac{1}{d_i^{in}\theta(v_i)} \sum_{v_j \in \eta_i^{in}} x_{j,t-1} \tag{3.7}$$

Proposition 3.1. *If V' is a solution to MIN-SEED, then setting $\forall v_i \in V', x_{i,1} = 1$ and $\forall v_i \notin V', x_{i,1} = 0$ is a solution to SEED-IP. If the vector $[x_{i,t}]$ is a solution to SEED-IP, then $\{v_i | x_{i,1} = 1\}$ is a solution to MIN-SEED.*

However, despite the availability of approximate solvers, SEED-IP requires a quadratic number of variables and constraints (Proposition 3.2), which likely will prevent this approach from scaling to very large datasets. As a result, in the next section we introduce our heuristic approach.

Proposition 3.2. *SEED-IP requires n^2 variables and $2n^2$ constraints.*

3.3.2   Heuristic

Next, we present the heuristic algorithm of [22, 23]. The algorithm is based on the idea of shell decomposition often cited in physics literature [2, 5, 12, 18] but modified to ensure that the resulting set will lead to all nodes being activated. The algorithm, TIP_DECOMP is presented in this section.

Intuitively, the algorithm proceeds as follows (Fig. 3.1). Given network $G = (V, E)$ where each node v_i has threshold $k_i = \lceil \theta(v_i) \cdot d_i^{in} \rceil$, at each iteration, pick the node for which $d_i^{in} - k_i$ is the least but positive (or 0) and remove it. Once there are no nodes for which $d_i^{in} - k_i$ is positive (or 0), the algorithm outputs the remaining nodes in the network. The resulting set of nodes is guaranteed to cause all nodes in the graph to activate under the tipping model.

Theorem 3.2. *If all nodes in $V' \subseteq V$ returned by TIP_DECOMP are initially active, then every node in V will eventually be activated, too.*

Algorithm 1 TIP_DECOMP

Require: Threshold function, θ and directed social network $G = (V, E)$
Ensure: V'

1: For each vertex v_i, compute k_i.
2: For each vertex v_i, $dist_i = d_i^{in} - k_i$.
3: FLAG = TRUE.
4: **while** FLAG **do**
5:      Let v_i be the element of v where $dist_i$ is minimal.
6:      **if** $dist_i = \infty$ **then**
7:          FLAG = FALSE.
8:      **else**
9:          Remove v_i from G and for each v_j in η_i^{out}, if $dist_j > 0$, set $dist_j = dist_j - 1$. Otherwise set $dist_j = \infty$.
10:     **end if**
11: **end whilereturn** All nodes left in G.

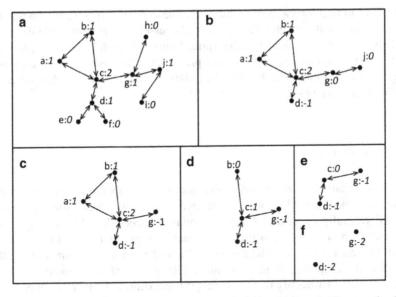

Fig. 3.1 Example of our algorithm for a simple network depicted in box **A**. We use a threshold value set to 50% of the node degree. Next to each node label (lower-case letter) is the value for $d_i^{in} - k_i$ (where $k_i = \lceil \frac{d_i^{in}}{2} \rceil$). In the first four iterations, nodes e, f, h, and i are removed resulting in the network in box **B**. This is followed by the removal of node j resulting in the network in box **C**. In the next two iterations, nodes a and b are removed (boxes **D-E** respectively). Finally, node c is removed (box **F**). The nodes of the final network, consisting of d and g, have negative values for $d_i - \theta_i$ and become the output of the algorithm

We also note that by using the appropriate data structure (we used a binomial heap in our implementation), for a network of n nodes and m edges, this algorithm can run in time $O(m \log n)$.

Proposition 3.3. *The complexity of TIP_DECOMP is $O(m \cdot \log(n))$.*

3.4 Experimental Findings

In this section we describe the results of an experimental evaluation. We describe the datasets we used for the experiments in Sect. 3.4.1. We evaluate the run-time of TIP_DECOMP in Sect. 3.4.2. In Sect. 3.4.3, we evaluate the size of the seed-set returned by the algorithm and we compare this to the seed size returned by known centrality measures in Sect. 3.4.4. We then study how the removal of high-degree nodes affects the results of the algorithm in Sect. 3.4.5.

The algorithm TIP_DECOMP was written using Python 2.6.6 in 200 lines of code that leveraged the NetworkX library available from http://networkx.lanl. gov/. The code used a binomial heap library written by Björn B. Brandenburg available from http://www.cs.unc.edu/~bbb/. The experiments were run on a computer equipped with an Intel X5677 Xeon Processor operating at 3.46 GHz with a 12 MB Cache running Red Hat Enterprise Linux version 6.1 and equipped with 70 GB of physical memory. All statistics presented in this section were calculated using R 2.13.1 (Source code for *TIP_DECOMP* is available at https://github.com/viralTipping/viralTipping).

3.4.1 Datasets

In total, we examined 36 networks: nine academic collaboration networks, three e-mail networks, and 24 networks extracted from social-media sites. The sites included general-purpose social-media (similar to Facebook or MySpace) as well as special-purpose sites (i.e. focused on sharing of blogs, photos, or video).

All datasets used in this chapter were obtained from one of four sources: the ASU Social Computing Data Repository, [20] the Stanford Network Analysis Project, [13] the University of Michigan, [15] and Universitat Rovira i Virgili [1]. Thirty one of the networks considered were symmetric—i.e. if a directed edge from vertex v to v' exists, there is also an edge from vertex v' to v. The networks are categorized by the results for the MIN-SEED experiments (explained later in this section). Additionally, we also looked at several non-symmetric (directed) networks and placed them in their own category. In what follows, we provide their real-world context.

3.4.1.1 Category A

- **BlogCatalog** is a social blog directory that allows users to share blogs with friends [20]. The first two samples of this site, BlogCatalog1 and 2, were taken in Jul. 2009 and June 2010 respectively. The third sample, BlogCatalog3 was uploaded to ASU's Social Computing Data Repository in Aug. 2010.
- **Buzznet** is a social media network designed for sharing photographs, journals, and videos [20]. It was extracted in Nov. 2010.
- **Douban** is a Chinese social medial website designed to provide user reviews and recommendations [20]. It was extracted in Dec. 2010.
- **Flickr** is a social media website that allows users to share photographs [20]. It was uploaded to ASU's Social Computing Data Repository in Aug. 2010.
- **Flixster** is a social media website that allows users to share reviews and other information about cinema [20]. It was extracted in Dec. 2010.
- **FourSquare** is a location-based social media site [20]. It was extracted in Dec. 2010.
- **Frienster** is a general-purpose social-networking site [20]. It was extracted in Nov. 2010.
- **Last.Fm** is a music-centered social media site [20]. It was extracted in Dec. 2010.

- **LiveJournal** is a site designed to allow users to share their blogs [20]. It was extracted in Jul. 2010.
- **Livemocha** is touted as the "world's largest language community" [20]. It was extracted in Dec. 2010.
- **WikiTalk** is a network of individuals who set and received messages while editing WikiPedia pages [13]. It was extracted in Jan. 2008.

3.4.1.2   Category B

- **Delicious** is a social bookmarking site, designed to allow users to share web bookmarks with their friends [20]. It was extracted in Dec. 2010.
- **Digg** is a social news website that allows users to share stories with friends [20]. It was extracted in Dec. 2010.
- **EU E-Mail** is an e-mail network extracted from a large European Union research institution [13]. It is based on e-mail traffic from Oct. 2003 to May 2005.
- **Hyves** is a popular general-purpose Dutch social networking site [20]. It was extracted in Dec. 2010.
- **Yelp** is a social networking site that allows users to share product reviews [20]. It was extracted in Nov. 2010.

3.4.1.3   Category C

- **CA-AstroPh** is a an academic collaboration network for Astro Physics from Jan. 1993 to Apr. 2003 [13].
- **CA-CondMat** is an academic collaboration network for Condense Matter Physics. Samples from 1999 (CondMat99), 2003 (CondMat03), and 2005 (Cond-Mat05) were obtained from the University of Michigan [15]. A second sample from 2003 (CondMat03a) was obtained from Stanford University [13].
- **CA-GrQc** is a an academic collaboration network for General Relativity and Quantum Cosmology from Jan. 1993 to Apr. 2003 [13].
- **CA-HepPh** is a an academic collaboration network for High Energy Physics - Phenomenology from Jan. 1993 to Apr. 2003 [13].
- **CA-HepTh** is a an academic collaboration network for High Energy Physics - Theory from Jan. 1993 to Apr. 2003 [13].
- **CA-NetSci** is a an academic collaboration network for Network Science from May 2006.
- **Enron E-Mail** is an e-mail network from the Enron corporation made public by the Federal Energy Regulatory Commission during its investigation [13].
- **URV E-Mail** is an e-mail network based on communications of members of the University Rovira i Virgili (Tarragona) [1]. It was extracted in 2003.
- **YouTube** is a video-sharing website that allows users to establish friendship links [20]. The first sample (YouTube1) was extracted in Dec. 2008. The second sample (YouTube2) was uploaded to ASU's Social Computing Data Repository in Aug. 2010.

Fig. 3.2 $m \ln n$ vs. runtime in seconds (log scale, m is number of edges, n is number of nodes). The relationship is linear with $R^2 = 0.9015$, $p = 2.2 \cdot 10^{-16}$

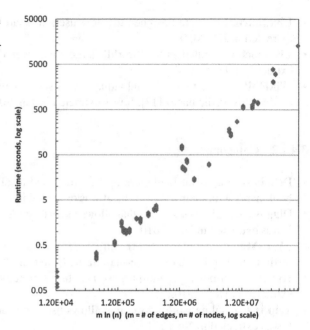

3.4.2   Runtime

First, we examined the runtime of the algorithm (see Fig. 3.2). Our experiments aligned well with our time complexity result (Proposition 3.3). For example, a network extracted from the Dutch social-media site Hyves consisting of 1.4 million nodes and 5.5 million directed edges was processed by our algorithm in at most 12.2 min. The often-cited LiveJournal dataset consisting of 2.2 million nodes and 25.6 million directed edges was processed in no more than 66 min—a short time to approximate an NP-hard combinatorial problem on a large-sized input.

3.4.3   Seed Size

For each network, we performed 10 "integer" trials. In these trials, we set $\theta(v_i) = \min(d_i^{in}, k)$ where k was kept constant among all vertices for each trial and set at an integer in the interval $[1, 10]$. We evaluated the ability of a network to promote spreading under the tipping model based on the size of the set of nodes returned by our algorithm (as a percentage of total nodes). For the purposes of discussion, we have grouped our networks into three categories based on results (Fig. 3.3a). In general, online social networks had the smallest seed sets—13 networks of this type had an average seed set size less than 2 % of the population (these networks were all

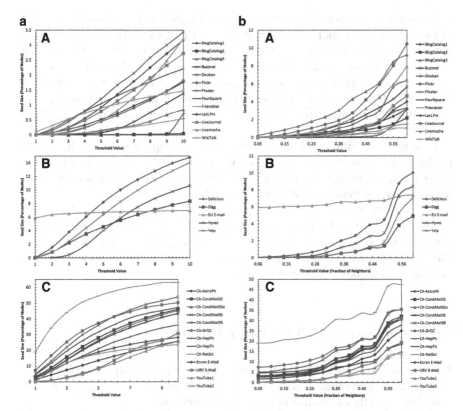

Fig. 3.3 Threshold value vs. size of initial seed the set as returned by our algorithm in our three identified categories of networks (categories A–C are depicted in panels A–C respectively). Figure on the left (**a**) has its threshold value assigned as an integer in the interval $[1, 10]$ whereas the right (**b**) one as a fraction of node in-degree as a multiple of 0.05 in the interval $[0.05, 0.60]$. In left figure (**a**), average seed sizes were under 2% for Category A, 2–10% for Category B and over 10% for Category C. The relationship, in general, was linear for categories A & B and logarithmic for C. CA-NetSci had the largest Louvain Modularity and clustering coefficient of all the networks. In the right figure (**b**), average seed sizes were under 5% for Category A, 17% for Category B and over 3% for Category C. The relationship between threshold and initial seed size for networks in all categories was exponential

in Category A). We also noticed, that for most networks, there was a linear relation between threshold value and seed size.

Category A can be thought of as social networks highly susceptible to influence—as a very small fraction of initially activated individuals can lead to activation of the entire population. All were extracted from social media websites. For some of the lower threshold levels, the size of the set of seed nodes was particularly small. For a threshold of three, 11 of the Category A networks produced seeds smaller than 0.5% of the total populations. For a threshold of four, nine networks met this criteria.

Networks in Category B are susceptible to influence with a relatively small set of initial nodes—but not to the extent of those in Category A. They had an average initial seed size greater than 2 % but less than 10 %. Members in this group included two general purpose social media networks, two specialty social media networks, and an e-mail network. Non-symmetric networks generally performed somewhat poorer than Category B networks (though in general, not as poorly as those in Category C). The initial seed sizes for the non-symmetric networks ranged from 3 to 29 %.

Category C consisted of networks that seemed to hamper diffusion in the tipping model, having an average initial seed size greater than 10 %. This category included all of the academic collaboration networks, two of the email networks, and two networks derived from friendship links on YouTube.

We also studied the effects on spreading when the threshold values were assigned as a specific fraction of each node's in-degree [10, 19], which results in heterogeneous θ_i's across the network. We performed 12 trials for each network. Thresholds for each trial were based on the product of in-degree and a fraction in the interval $[0.05, 0.60]$ (multiples of 0.05).

3.4.4   Comparison with Centrality Measures

We compared our results with six popular centrality measures: degree, betweenness, closeness, shell number, eigenvector, and PageRank. Here, we define degree centrality is simply the number of outgoing adjacent nodes.

We evaluated the performance of centrality measures in finding a seed set by iteratively selecting the most central nodes with respect to a given measure until the Γ_θ of that set returns the set of all nodes. Due to the computational overhead of calculating these centrality measures and the repeated re-evaluation of Γ_θ, we limited this comparison to only **BlogCatalog3**, **CA-HepTh**, **CA-NetSci**, **URV E-Mail**, and **Douban** (no betweeness calculated for **Douban**). As with the experiments in the previous section, we studied threshold settings based on an integer in the interval $[1, 10]$ (see Fig. 3.4) and analogous results were found for the case where the thresholds were set as a fraction of nodes. In general, selecting highly-central nodes is an inefficient method for finding small seed sets.

In all but the lowest threshold settings, the use of centrality measures for the integer-threshold trials proved to significantly underperformed when the method presented in this chapter—often returning seed-sets several orders of magnitude larger and in many cases including the majority of nodes in the network. Even for the centrality measures which outperform our method in these trials, the reduction in seed set size was minimal (the greatest reduction in seed set size experienced in a centrality-measure test over the algorithm of this chapter was 0.09 %, while often producing seed sets orders of magnitude greater than our method). This held even for the centrality measures associated with diffusion (shell number, eigenvector, and PageRank).

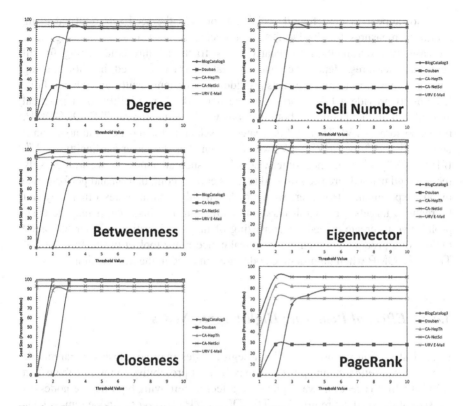

Fig. 3.4 The use of degree, shell number, betweenness, Eigenvector, closeness and PageRank to find seed-sets on select networks when the threshold is set to an integer in the interval $[1, 10]$

Our tests using fractional-based thresholds tell a slightly different story. While our method still generally outperformed the centrality measures for the fractional tests, there were a few cases where the centrality measures fared better. With **BlogCatalog3** all of the centrality measures outperformed our algorithm in the fraction-based experiments. For that dataset, centrality-based algorithm consistently outperformed our method finding seed sets with less members (by 3.13–3.29 % of the population, on average). With **URV-Email**, many trials that utilized a lower threshold setting outperformed our method, but never finding a seed set with smaller by more than 8 % of the total population. However, in the larger threshold settings, our method consistently found smaller seeds. For a given centrality measure for this dataset, centrality measures on average provided poorer results than our algorithm ranged—returning seed sets which were, on average 10.22–67.14 % (by overall population) larger than that returned by our algorithm. Perhaps the most interesting result among the centrality measures were the PageRank fraction-based tests on **CA-NetSci**, which is associated with the largest seed sets. PageRank found seed sets that were, on average 14.45 % smaller (by population) than our approach. Additionally, though centrality measures outperformed TIP_DECOMP for **BlogCatalog3**, this does not appear to hold for all social networks as the seed sets returned using centrality measures for the Douban approaches at least an order of magnitude increase over our method for nearly every fractional threshold setting for all centrality measures. Hence, we conclude that for fraction-based thresholds, using centrality measures to find seed sets provides inconsistent results, and when it fails, it tends to provide a large portion of the network. A possibility for a practical algorithm that could combine both methods would be to first run TIP_DECOMP, returning some set V'. Then, V'' is created by selecting the most central nodes until either $|V'| = |V''|$ or $\Gamma_\theta(V'') = V$ (whichever ensures the lower cardinality for V''. If $|V'| = |V''|$, V' is returned, otherwise V''. For such an approach, we would likely recommend using degree centrality due to its ease of computation and performance in our experiments. However, we note that highly-central nodes often may not be realistic targets for a viral-marketing campaign. For instance, it may be cost-prohibitive to create a seed set consisting of major celebrities in order to spread the use of a product. As such is a practical concern, we look at the performance of TIP_DECOMP when high-degree nodes are removed in the next section.

3.4.5   Effect of Removing High-Degree Nodes

In the last section we noted that high-degree nodes may not always be targetable in a viral marketing campaign (i.e. it may be cost prohibitive to include them in a seed set). In this section, we explore the affect of removing high-degree nodes on the size of the seed-set returned by TIP_DECOMP. This type of node removal has also recently been studied in a different context in [4]. In these trials, we studied all 31 networks and looked at two specific threshold settings: an integer threshold of 2 (Fig. 3.5) and analogous results were found with respect to fractional threshold. We then studied the effect of removing up to 50 % of the nodes in order from greatest to least degree.

With an integer threshold of 2, networks in category A still retained a seed-size (as returned by TIP_DECOMP) two orders of magnitude smaller than the population size up to the removal of 10 % of the top degree nodes, and for many networks this was maintained to 50 %. Networks in category B retained seed sets an order of magnitude smaller than the population for up to 50 % of the nodes removed. For most networks in category C, the seed size remained about a quarter of the population size up to 15 % of the top degree nodes being removed.

With a fractional threshold of 0.5, we noted that many networks in category A actually had larger seed sets (as returned by TIP_DECOMP) when more high degree nodes are removed. Further, networks in categories A-B retained seed sets of at least an order of magnitude smaller than the population in these tests while most networks in category C retained sizes of about a quarter of the population.

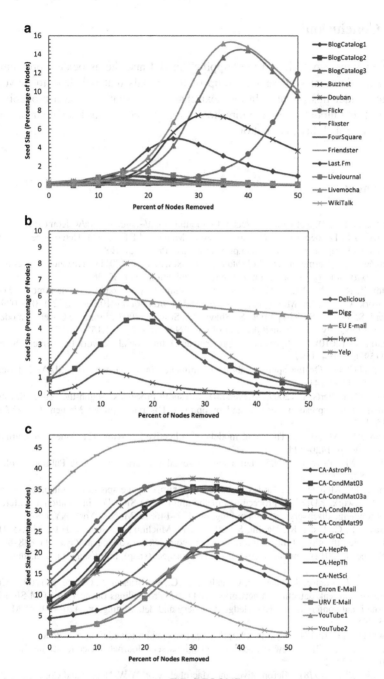

Fig. 3.5 Size of the seed set returned by TIP_DECOMP (as a fraction of the population) as a function of the percentage of the highest degree nodes removed from the network with an integer threshold of 2 for networks in categories A–C

3.5 Conclusion

In this chapter, we reviewed the "tipping" model and the associated problem of finding a minimum seed set—a group of individuals that will lead to universal adoption under this process. In the next chapter, we shall look at a probabilistic variant of this model where the threshold for each node is not known but selected based on a probability distribution.

References

1. Arenas, A. (2012). Network data sets. http://deim.urv.cat/~aarenas/data/welcome.htm
2. Baxter, G.J., Dorogovtsev, S.N., Goltsev, A.V., Mendes, J.F.F. (2011). Heterogeneous k-core versus bootstrap percolation on complex networks . Phys. Rev. E 83.
3. Ben-Zwi, O., Hermelin, D., Lokshtanov, D., Newman, I. (2011). Treewidth governs the complexity of target set selection. Discrete Optimization 8 (1), 87–96.
4. Boldi, P., Rosa, M., Vigna, S.: Robustness of social and web graphs to node removal. Social Network Analysis and Mining pp. 1–14 (2013). http://dx.doi.org/10.1007/s13278-013-0096-x
5. Carmi, S., Havlin, S., Kirkpatrick, S., Shavitt, Y., Shir, E. (2007). From the Cover: A model of Internet topology using k-shell decomposition. PNAS 104 (27), 11,150–11,154.
6. Centola, D. (2010). The Spread of Behavior in an Online Social Network Experiment. Science 329 (5996), 1194–1197.
7. Chen, N.(2009) On the approximability of influence in social networks. SIAM J. Discrete Math. 23, 1400–1415.
8. Dreyer, P., Roberts, F. (2009). Irreversible -threshold processes: Graph-theoretical threshold models of the spread of disease and of opinion. Discrete Applied Mathematics 157 (7), 1615–1627.
9. Granovetter, M. (1978). Threshold models of collective behavior. The American Journal of Sociology (6), 1420–1443.
10. Jackson, M., Yariv, L. (2005). Diffusion on social networks. Economie Publique, vol. 16, pp. 69–82.
11. Kempe, D., Kleinberg, J., Tardos, E. (2003). Maximizing the spread of influence through a social network. KDD '03: Proceedings of the ninth ACM SIGKDD international conference on Knowledge discovery and data mining, pp. 137–146. ACM, New York, NY, USA.
12. Kitsak, M., Gallos, L.K., Havlin, S., Liljeros, F., Muchnik, L., Stanley, H.E., Makse, H.A. (2010). Identification of influential spreaders in complex networks. Nat Phys (11), 888–893.
13. Leskovec, J. (2012). Stanford network ana lysis project (snap). http://snap.stanford.edu/index.html
14. Leskovec, J., Krause, A., Guestrin, C., Faloutsos, C., VanBriesen, J., Glance, N. (2007). Cost-effective outbreak detection in networks. KDD '07: Proceedings of the 13th ACM SIGKDD international conference on Knowledge discovery and data mining, pp. 420–429. ACM, New York, NY, USA.
15. Newman, M.(2011) Network data. http://www-personal.umich.edu/~mejn/netdata/
16. Reichman, D. (2012). New bounds for contagious sets. Journal, Discrete Mathematics 312 (10), (May 2012).
17. Schelling, T.C. (1978). Micromotives and Macrobehavior. W.W. Norton and Co.
18. Seidman, S.B. (1983). Network structure and minimum degree. Social Networks 5 (3), 269–287.
19. Watts, D.J., Dodds, P.S. (2007) Influentials, networks, and public opinion formation. Journal of Consumer Research 34 (4), 441–458. http://www.journals.uchicago.edu/doi/abs/10.1086/518527

20. Zafarani, R., Liu, H. (2009). Social computing data repository at ASU . http://socialcomputing. asu.edu
21. Zhang, L., Marbach, P. (2011). Two is a crowd: Optimal trend adoption in social networks. Proceedings of International Conference on Game Theory for Networks (GameNets)
22. P. Shakarian, S. Eyre, D. Paulo. A Scalable Heuristic for Viral Marketing Under the Tipping Model. Social Network Analysis and Mining. Springer 3(4), 2013.
23. P. Shakarian, D. Paulo. Large Social Networks can be Targeted for Viral Marketing with Small Seed Sets. 2012 IEEE/ACM International Conference on Advances in Social Networks Analysis and Mining (ASONAM-2012) (Aug. 2012).

Chapter 4
The Independent Cascade and Linear Threshold Models

4.1 Introduction

In Chaps. 2 and 3, we presented the SIR model and the tipping model respectively. In the former any node infected in last time step has a single chance (with probability β, a parameter of the model) to infect any of its neighbors which are not in a susceptible state. In the latter, an individual adopts a behavior if it has certain number of adopted incoming neighbors.

In this chapter, we focus on independent cascade (IC) model which is a generalized of SIR model, and two other models known as linear threshold (LT) and generalized threshold (GT) models, which are probabilistic extensions of the tipping model. These models are similar to the tipping dynamics of Chap. 3, except that the tipping threshold for each node is drawn at random.

In this chapter, we describe properties of these models and study problems of influence maximization and spread in this context. Finally, we present approaches to address the influence maximization problem to find the seed sets that maximize the number of adopters in expectation.

4.2 Model Definitions

We assume a social network $G = (V, E)$, where V is a set of vertices and E is a set of directed edges. For a given node $v \in V$, the set of incoming neighbors and outgoing neighbors are considered as $\eta^{in}(v)$ and $\eta^{out}(v)$ respectively. We will use the notation $|\cdot|$ for the cardinality of the sets.

The diffusion process occurs in discrete time steps t. If a node adopts a new behaviour or idea, it becomes active, otherwise it is inactive. An inactive node has the ability to become active. The set of active nodes at time t is considered as $\mathcal{X}_t$. The tendency of an inactive node v to become active is positively correlated with the

© The Author(s) 2015
P. Shakarian et al., *Diffusion in Social Networks*, SpringerBriefs
in Computer Science, DOI 10.1007/978-3-319-23105-1_4

number of active incoming neighbors v. Also, we assume that each node can only switch from inactive state to active state, and an active node will remain active for the rest of the diffusion process—hence these models are often referred to as "progressive" or "montonic." On the other hand, in non-progressive models active nodes can also switch back and become inactive—we will cover these in Chap. 6 when we describe evolutionary graph theory. In general, we start with an initial seed set $\mathscr{X}_0$ (when it is clear from context, we shall often drop the subscript and use $\mathscr{X}$ to denote the seed set), and through the diffusion process, for a given inactive node v, its active neighbors attempt to activate it. The process runs until no more activations occur.

4.2.1   Independent Cascade Model

Independent cascade (IC) model generalizes the SIR model described in Chap. 2. Instead of a single probability infection, there is a probability of infection associated with each edge. The probability $P_{u,v}$ is the probability of u infecting v. This probability can be assigned based on frequency of interactions, geographic proximity, or historical infection traces. Each node, once infected, has the ability to infect its neighbor in the next time step based on the probability associated with that edge.

Definition 4.1 (Independent Cascade Model (IC)). Under the Independent Cascade model dynamics, at each time step t where $\mathscr{X}_{t-1}^{new}$ is the set of *newly* activated nodes at time $t-1$, each $v \in \mathscr{X}_{t-1}^{new}$ infects the inactive neighbors $u \in \eta^{out}(v)$ with a probability $P_{u,v}$.

An example of this model is shown in Fig. 4.1. Active nodes are shown in yellow dotted line. At initial time, two nodes C and D are activated. At the next time step, node C and D has a chance to activate their three neighbors (A, G, and H) and (B, E, and F) respectively. According to Fig. 4.1b, only three nodes A, H, and E are successfully activated and the initial active nodes change to gray (denoting it stays active but no chance to activate others). In the next time step, two nodes G and F become active, and the previous active nodes A, E, and H change to gray. At time $t = 2$, two nodes F and G become active. Node G's neighbors are active, so it does not have a chance to activate any nodes. Node F has an option to activate node I; however it fails as shown in our given example in Fig. 4.1d. Since there is no more new active node, the diffusion process stopped.

4.2.2   Linear Threshold Model

The linear threshold model extends tipping model to its natural, weighted variant where each directed edge $(u,v) \in E$ has a non-negative weight $b(u,v)$. For any node $v \in V$, the total incoming edge weights sum to less than or equal to one, i.e. $\sum_{u \in \eta^{in}(v)} b(u,v) \leq 1$. The dynamics of the model are specified below.

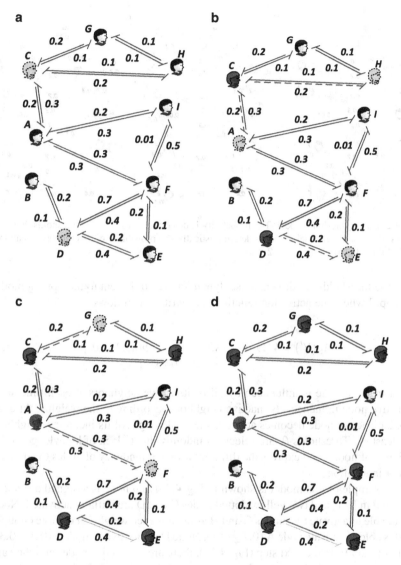

Fig. 4.1 Independent cascade model. Probability of transitions from each state to its successor state(in alphabetic order) are 7.0^{-3}, 6.0^{-3}, 5.0^{-1}, and 1.0, respectively. The probability of occurring for this sequence is 2.0^{-5}. (**a**) $t = 0$. (**b**) $t = 1$. (**c**) $t = 2$. (**d**) $t = 3$

Definition 4.2 (Linear Threshold Model (LT)). Under the linear threshold model dynamics, each node v selects a threshold θ_v in the interval $[0,1]$ uniformly at random. Then, at each time step t where H_{t-1} is the set of nodes activated at time $t-1$ or earlier, each inactive node becomes active if $\sum_{u \in \eta^{in}(v) \cap H_{t-1}} b(u,v) \geq \theta_v$.

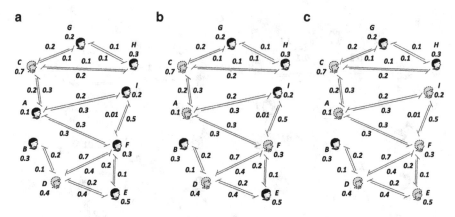

Fig. 4.2 Linear threshold model. The probability is determined based on the thresholds drawn at the first step, then the model proceeds deterministically.The probability of this sequence is almost 7.0^{-3}. (**a**) $t = 0$. (**b**) $t = 1$. (**c**) $t = 2$

Once the thresholds are drawn, these dynamics are equivalent to the tipping model of Chap. 3 where the activation function is re-written as follows:

$$A_\theta(V') = V' \cup \{v \in V s.t. \sum_{u \in \eta^{in}(v) \cap V'} b(u,v) \geq \theta_v\} \qquad (4.1)$$

An inactive node is influenced by all of its active neighbors at each time step. An active node influences its inactive neighbors according to the weights. At each step, an inactive node becomes active if the total weight of its incoming neighbors is at least θ_v. Thresholds θ_v are selected randomly due to lack of knowledge of the tendency of nodes, and express the different levels of tendency of nodes to adopt an idea or innovation.

An example of this model is shown in Fig. 4.2. Each node is assigned a random threshold in [0,1] and two yellow dotted nodes C and D are initially activated. Node C is unable to activate two nodes G and H as its influence weight is not large enough, but it is able to activate node A ($0.2 \geq 0.1$). Node D also activates node F ($0.4 \geq 0.3$), but not B and E. In the next step (Fig. 4.2b), there are four active nodes and they are able to activate node I ($0.3 + 0.5 \geq 0.2$) and E ($0.4 + 0.2 \geq 0.5$). In the next time step, no new active node exists; so, the diffusion process terminates.

4.2.3 Generalized Threshold Model

Generalized threshold model is a broader framework of which the linear threshold and independent cascade models are special cases. Kempe et al. [1] also presented a generalized cascade model, which is equivalent to generalized threshold model. Therefore, we only provide the generalized threshold model definition here.

Definition 4.3 (Generalized Threshold Model (GT)). Given node v, a monotone threshold function $f_v : 2^{\eta^{in}(v)} \to [0,1]$, a threshold value $\theta_v \in [0,1]$, and an active set $\mathscr{X}_t$ at time t, node v is infected at time step t if $f_v(\mathscr{X}_t) \geq \theta_v$.

Again, the threshold value θ_v is uniformly randomly chosen for each node v. Linear threshold model is a special case of generalized threshold model, where the threshold function is in the form of summation over all active neighbors of node v, denoted $\mathscr{X}^v$, i.e. $f_v(\mathscr{X}^v) = \sum_{u \in \mathscr{X}^v} b(u,v)$ where $\sum_{u \in \eta_v^{in}} b(u,v) \leq 1$.

4.3 Influence Maximization Problem

In this section, we examine the influence maximization problem for the previously-mentioned models. First, we introduce some common terminology and concepts among all three models. The diffusion models involve an initial set of nodes to start. The *influence* of an initial set is defined as the number of active nodes at the end of the diffusion process. This is often referred to as *influence spread*.

Definition 4.4 (Influence Spread). Given an initial seed set $\mathscr{X}$, influence spread is the expected number of infectees $\sigma(\mathscr{X})$.

A natural optimization problem is to find the set of maximum influence nodes with a specific size k. That is, the initial k-node set $\mathscr{X}$ has been targeted to become active. We can formally define this problem as:

Definition 4.5 (Influence Maximization Problem). Given a natural number k, find an initial seed set $\mathscr{X}$, where $|\mathscr{X}| \leq k$, such that $\sigma(\mathscr{X})$ is maximized.

Unfortunately, this problem is NP-hard. This reduction is shown by an embedding of the max-k-cover problem.

In 1978, Nemhauser et al. [2] showed that (under the assumption that the influence spread can be efficiently calculated) a greedy algorithm provides an $(1 - 1/e)$ approximation if f meets normalization, monotonicity and submodularity conditions.

Definition 4.6 (Normalization). If there is no initial infectees then there is no spread, i.e. $f(\emptyset) = 0$.

Definition 4.7 (Montonicity). For $S \subseteq S', f(S) \leq f(S')$.

Definition 4.8 (Submodularity). An arbitrary set function $f : S \to \mathbb{R}$ is submodular if and only if for all $S', S'' \subseteq S$, it is the case that if $S' \subseteq S''$, then $f(S' \cup \{s\}) - f(S') \geq f(S'' \cup \{s\}) - f(S'')$. Intuitively, a submodular function has diminishing returns property.

The intuition behind submodularity can be explained with the following example. Suppose you have a poor man with very few possessions (H_1) and a rich man with many more possessions (H_2). Suppose neither possesses a Ferrari car (h). Giving the poor man the Ferrari would make a greater difference to his net worth (computed via f as a function of the person's possessions) than giving it to the rich man.

4.3.1   Influence Maximization Under the IC Model

Kempe et al. [1] show that influence maximization problem can be viewed as a general case of an NP-complete Set Cover problem under the IC model.

Theorem 4.1 (Complexity of Influence Maximization in the IC Model). *The influence maximization in the independent cascade model is NP-hard within a factor of $1 - 1/e + \varepsilon$ for any $\varepsilon > 0$.*

They [1] also show that σ meets the requirements (mentioned under Definition 4.6, 4.7 and 4.8) under the IC model.

Theorem 4.2. *In the independent cascade model, the influence function $\sigma_{IC}(\cdot)$ is normalized, monotone, and submodular.*

We will give an intuition for this finding under IC dynamics. The influence function in IC is normalized, since if there is no initial infectees then there is no spread, i.e. $\sigma_{IC}(\emptyset) = 0$. It is also monotone, because each element of $\mathscr{X}$ contributes at least one expected infectee. However, this is not true if we do not count nodes in set $\mathscr{X}$ toward the expected infectees. In this case, we can view the oracle function as $\sigma_{IC}(\mathscr{X}) - |\mathscr{X}|$, which is not monotonic. This is a special case of *profit maximization* [6, 7].

We can prove submodularity of the influence function in IC model using live-edge model. The proof of submodularity relies on a manipulation of the "live edge" model—a mathematically equivalent representation of the IC model (and several others as well). This technique is commonly used in much of the literature relating to the models described in this chapter. We outline the technique used to obtain this result next.

First, we define an *outcome* under the IC models as a subgraph of G. A given outcome intuitively is one possible way the IC process can occur. Using this idea, we can assign a probability to an outcome as follows. For outcome $G' = (V, E')$ the probability of the outcome is: $\Pi_{(u,v) \in E'} P_{u,v} \times \Pi_{(u,v) \in E \setminus E'}(1 - Pu, v)$. For a given outcome $\mathscr{W}$, we denote this probability $Pr(\mathscr{W})$.

Definition 4.9 (Live-Edge Path). Given graph G, and an initial active set $\mathscr{X}$, the path from $\mathscr{X}$ to other nodes is called a live-edge path.

According to the definition, given graph G with edge probabilities, we can view some subgraph G' as a potential set of available edges that diffusion can deterministically occur.

Definition 4.10 (Live-Edge Model). Given graph $G = (V, E)$, seed set $\mathscr{X}$, and probability distribution Pr over subgraphs of G, the probability a node $v \in V \setminus \mathscr{X}$ is defined as the sum of the probabilities of subgraphs of G (based on Pr) where exists a path from a node in $\mathscr{X}$ to v is active.

As, for a given subgraph G', the infection is deterministic, a node x is infected under the live-edge model if there is simply a path from a node in $\mathscr{X}$ to x. The edges successfully activate are declared as *live*, and the rest of the edges are declared as *blocked*. Kempe et al. show that live-edge model is equivalent to IC model.

Algorithm 2 Greedy Algorithm

1: **procedure** GREEDYAPPROXIMATION(V, k)
2:     Set $\mathscr{X} = \emptyset$
3:     **while** $|\mathscr{X}| \leq k$ **do**
4:         Pick $s \in V$ where $\sigma(\mathscr{X} \cup s) - \sigma(\mathscr{X})$ is the greatest
5:         Add s to $\mathscr{X}$
6:     **end while**
7:     **return** $\mathscr{X}$
8: **end procedure**

Consider two sets S and S' such that $S \subseteq S'$ and an element s which is in neither. For random weight of edges $\mathscr{W}$, Let $R_{\mathscr{W}}(S)$, $R_{\mathscr{W}}(S')$, and $R_{\mathscr{W}}(\{s\})$ be the sets of nodes reachable by S, S', and s by weights $\mathscr{W}$, respectively. Since $|R_{\mathscr{W}}(S') \cap R_{\mathscr{W}}(\{s\})| \geq |R_{\mathscr{W}}(S) \cap R_{\mathscr{W}}(\{s\})|$; thus, $\sigma_{\mathscr{W}}(S \cup \{s\}) - \sigma_{\mathscr{W}}(S) \geq \sigma_{\mathscr{W}}(S' \cup \{s\}) - \sigma_{\mathscr{W}}(S')$. For any $\mathscr{W}$, we have the following relationship: $\sigma_{IC}(S) = \sum_{\mathscr{W}} Pr(\mathscr{W}) \times \sigma_{\mathscr{W}}(S)$ As positive linear combinations of submodular functions are also submodular, we have completed the proof.

Greedy Approximation Algorithm To find the initial seed set we can use *Greedy Algorithm* as presented in Algorithm 2. In each iteration, the element with maximum marginal influence is added to the seed set. Let k be the size of the seed set, there are k and $|V|$ iterations of the outer loop and inner loop respectively, where each of these $k \times |V|$ iterations require many evaluations of σ. Thus, this becomes very expensive. And note, this assumes that the computation of σ can be done efficiently. However, the straight-forward method is to rely on simulation, which is also expensive.

Let us consider the issue of the calculation of σ. It turns out, that by leveraging the live-edge model, that calculation influence is #P-hard by a reduction from the counting version of *s-t* connectivity (this result was originally proven by Chen et al. in [5]). The problem of *s-t* connectivity deals with determining if their exist a path between two nodes (denoted s and t) in a graph. Chen's reduction works by creating an instance of the live-edge model where the probability of t adopting given a seed set consisting of node s is proportional to the number of paths between these two nodes.

Theorem 4.3 (Complexity of Influence Spread in the IC Model). *In the independent cascade model, influence spread $\sigma_{IC}(\cdot)$ is #P-hard.*

Practically, we can obtain arbitrarily close approximation using simulation. However, this is expensive and at the time of this writing, does not provide any formal guarantee.

However, the expected number of infectees is solvable in polynomial time for directed acyclic graphs [5]. We can compute the activation probability, the probability of a node u is infected given seed set $\mathscr{X}$, of each node using Algorithm 3. Though this seems to be a restrictive case, this intuition is useful in building a heuristic approach to this problem—as we shall describe later in the chapter.

Algorithm 3 Computing Activation Probability in DAG

1: **procedure** ACTIVATIONPROBABILTY($D, \mathcal{X}$)
2:    $\forall u \in$ DAG $D, ap(u) = 0$
3:    $\forall u \in$ seed set $\mathcal{X}, ap(u) = 1$
4:    Topologically sort all nodes reachable from $\mathcal{X}$ in D into a sequence ρ, with in-degree zero nodes sorted first.
5:    **for** $u \in \{\rho \setminus \mathcal{X}\}$ according to the order ρ **do**
6:        $ap(u) = \sum_{x \in \eta^{in}(u) \cap \rho} ap(x) \times b(x, u)$
7:    **end for**
8:    **return** S
9: **end procedure**

4.3.2 Influence Maximization Under the LT Model

We now turn our attention to influence maximization and influence spread under the LT model. It turns out that influence spread calculation is also #P-hard [4]. This time the proof is shown by a reduction from the problem of counting the number of simple paths between nodes—again using the live-edge model.

Theorem 4.4 (Complexity of Influence Spread in the LT Model). *In the linear threshold model, influence spread $\sigma_{LT}(\cdot)$ is #P-hard.*

Further, even if influence spread can be computed efficiently, solving the influence maximization problem under this model is NP-hard by an embedding of the vertex cover problem [1].

Theorem 4.5 (Complexity of Influence Maximization in the LT Model). *The influence maximization in the linear threshold model is NP-hard.*

However, with respect to the optimization problem associated with influence maximization under LT, the same properties hold as with the IC model. Intuitively, the LT model is normalized (no seed, no diffusion). Monotonicity of the LT model follows the same argument showed for the IC model. Kempe et al. leverage the live-edge model and show that the model is submodular.

Theorem 4.6. *In the linear threshold model, the influence function $\sigma_{LT}(\cdot)$ is normalized, monotone, and submodular.*

4.3.3 Influence Maximization Under the GT Model

In [1] the generalized threshold model is shown to capture both the IC and LT models, hence the hardness results for both influence maximization and influence spread still hold.

Theorem 4.7 (Complexity of Influence Maximization in the GT Model). *The influence maximization in the generalized threshold model is NP-hard.*

Theorem 4.8 (Complexity of Influence Spread in the GT Model). *In the generalized threshold model, computing influence function $\sigma_{GT}(\cdot)$ is #P-hard.*

The influence maximization problem in GT model can be reduced to max-k-cover problem. It is NP-hard within a factor of $|V|^{1-\varepsilon}$ [1]. However, the result of Mossel and Roch [3] relate the local activation functions to influence spread, providing for an elegant result that allows the greedy algorithm to obtain an approximation guarantee in this large special case.

Theorem 4.9. *If all the activation functions are normalized, monotonic, and submodular, then the expected number of infectees under the generalized threshold model is also normalized, monotonic, and submodular [3].*

4.4 Scaling Influence Maximization

Due to the demands of potential real-world applications, Influence maximization problem should be scalable for the real world—as these are often of size 10^5 nodes or greater (i.e. see the datasets described in Chaps. 2 and 3). As we said in the previous section (Algorithm 2), Greedy algorithm is computationally expensive since in each iteration, it iterates through all the nodes in the given network, and we run the simulation multiple times to get a closer approximation of the diffusion outcome. In this section, we present two algorithms and one model to find the seed set with maximum influence for the LT and IC models.

4.4.1 Lazy Greedy Approximation

We can accelerate greedy algorithm and reduce its computational complexity under the certain assumption. In 1978, Minoux [8] showed that if a given function f is submodular, we can optimally accelerate greedy algorithms which is confirmed theoretically.

The key intuition behind "Lazy Greedy" algorithm is that by the definition of submodularity, the incremental increase to σ afforded by a node is always bounded above by its incremental increase on previous iterations. By checking this, we can avoid unnecessary calculation.

Consider the ith iteration of the Greedy Algorithm 2. Let $\mathcal{X}_i$ be the set of elements picked at the end of iteration $i - 1$. For node s, the algorithm evaluates the following quantity:

$$\lambda(i,s) = \sigma(\mathcal{X}_i \cup s) - \sigma(\mathcal{X}_i) \tag{4.2}$$

Let us call $\lambda(i,s)$ the incremental increase afforded to s at iteration i. Now, there are many nodes evaluated at a given iteration. Let us assume that s does not do very well—in fact it is somewhere in the middle of the pack. Now consider the $(i+1)^{th}$ iteration of the Greedy Algorithm. Let $\mathscr{X}_{i+1}$ be the set of elements picked at the end of iteration i. For node s, the algorithm evaluates the following quantity:

$$\lambda(i+1,s) = \sigma(\mathscr{X}_{i+1} \cup s) - \sigma(\mathscr{X}_{i+1}) \tag{4.3}$$

This value is incremental increase afforded to s at iteration $i+1$. Let us assume that s again does not do very well. We note that $\mathscr{X}_{i+1}$ is a superset of S_i. Hence, as $\sigma(\cdot)$ is submodular, we get the following:

$$\sigma(\mathscr{X}_{i+1} \cup s) - \sigma(\mathscr{X}_{i+1}) \leq \sigma(\mathscr{X}_i \cup s) - \sigma(\mathscr{X}_i) \tag{4.4}$$

$$\lambda(i+1,s) \leq \lambda(i,s) \tag{4.5}$$

So, suppose at iteration i we saved $\lambda(i,s)$ in some data structure. Suppose we start evaluating $\lambda(i+1,s)$ at the start of iteration $i+1$, and let s' be the node where currently $\lambda(i+1,s')$ is the greatest. So, now instead of evaluating $\lambda(i+1,s)$ directly, we perform the following steps:

1. If $\lambda(i+1,s') \leq \lambda(i,s)$:

   a. Evaluate $\lambda(i+1,s)$
   b. If $\lambda(i+1,s') \leq \lambda(i+1,s)$, then s is the node that affords the greatest incremental increase

2. Otherwise:

   a. Go to the next node

This can produce significant speedup in practice. Performance may vary depending on the ordering of the nodes and ordering the nodes may increase algorithm runtime. So, worst-case time complexity does not change. This algorithm also needs to iterate through all nodes during the first iteration of the outer loop.

To avoid costly simulation runs, we turn to the issue of scaling the computation of σ. In general, the approaches presented in the literature for scaling σ is tied to the underlying model, i.e. IC vs. LT. Hence, we shall describe a method for IC and a method for LT.

4.4.2 Maximum Influence Arborescence (MIA) Model

Computing the influence spread in the IC model is # P-hard, yet computable in polynomial time for directed trees. Chen et al. [5] introduce the maximum influence arborescence (MIA) model where the probability that node v' infects node v is based on the probability of v' infecting v only by the most influential path, called the *maximum influence path*. An arborescence is a directed tree with a root node v and for any other node v' there is exactly one directed path from v' to v.

For a given pair of nodes, $(u,v) \in E$, the MIA model is defined as the path between two nodes whose probability is greatest, denoted $MIP(u,v)$. If there is no path, then $MIP(u,v) = \emptyset$. This is uniquely and consistently determined for each node pair—hence ties are assumed to be broken in a consistent manner. If we create an alternative graph where each edge (u,v) is weighted by $\log(P(u,v)^{-1})$ then we can easily find the MIP's using Dijkstra's algorithm.

For a given node v, and a threshold $\theta \in [0,1]$, we define its *maximum influence in-arborescence* (MIIA)—the arborescence created by the union of all maximum influence paths starting from each other node to v whose probability exceeds threshold θ as follows:

$$MIIA(v,\theta) = \cup_{u \in V, Pr(MIP(u,v)) \geq \theta} MIP(u,v) \tag{4.6}$$

This is the graph created by the union of all MIP's from other nodes to v whose probability is at least θ. By keeping the MIP unique and consistently defined, we know the resulting graph is an arborescence. Note that this can be computed before any algorithmic attempt to solve the maximum influence problem.

Given a seed set $\mathcal{X}$, node u and an arborescence A, the activation probability $ap(u, \mathcal{X}, A)$ is the probability u is infected given seed set $\mathcal{X}$ in graph A under the IC model. There are three cases: 1) If u is in $\mathcal{X}$, then $ap(u, \mathcal{X}, A) = 1$, 2) If u is not in $\mathcal{X}$ and has no incoming neighbors, then $ap(u, \mathcal{X}, A) = 0$, 3) If the first two cases do not hold, then:

$$ap(u, \mathcal{X}, A) = 1 - \prod_{w \in \eta^{in}(u)} 1 - (ap(w, \mathcal{X}, A)) \times P(w,v)) \tag{4.7}$$

This can be computed in polynomial time by a single traversal of A by considering nodes from the leaves to the root.

Let the activation of node v given seed set $\mathcal{X}$ and its MIIA $ap(u, \mathcal{X}, MIIA(u,\theta))$, the expected number of infectees in the MIA model, denoted σ_M, given seed set $\mathcal{X}$ is computed as follows:

$$\sigma_M(\mathcal{X}) = \sum_{v \in V} ap(u, \mathcal{X}, MIIA(u,\theta)) \tag{4.8}$$

Note that the graph used to calculate the activation probability for each node can be different. As the activation probabilities can be computed in polynomial time, so can the expected number of infectees.

As we said, the goal is to replace the IC model with the MIA model in the algorithm in the hope that the seed set returned provides a large number of infectees (in expectation) under the IC model. Influence maximization problem under the MIA model is NP-hard. However, this problem becomes easier than influence maximization under the IC model, which, due to the difficulty of the influence spread problem, is actually harder [9] showed that this problem is actually #P hard. This NP-completeness result is due to the fact that influence spread under this model is computable in PTIME (see Algorithm 2). This also allows us to avoid costly simulation runs. Further, the MIA model is normalized, monotonic and submodular. So, the greedy algorithm can be applied and achieve the $1 - 1/e$ approximation ratio with respect to the expected number of infectees under the MIA model. The greedy algorithm for the MIA model possess no (known) theoretical properties with respect to the IC model though a close relationship has been shown experimentally. However, we note that the results with respect to the MIA model hold if we use lazy evaluation.

Chen et al. [5] demonstrate speedups to improve incremental increase specific to the MIA model. Suppose we are considering node w on the ith iteration of the greedy algorithm. When we compute the activation probability of some node v, the shortest path from w to v has a node previously picked. This causes an incremental increase of node w to be zero with regards to v. So, the intuition is at each iteration, re-compute the in-arborescence for each node such that no paths from other nodes outside of $\mathscr{X}$ contain a node in $\mathscr{X}$.

Chen et al. create a prefix-excluding variant of the MIA model, called PMIA. They defined a special version of MIIA, called PMIIA, that takes the current seed set into account. Then they identify extensions to monotonicity and submodularity and show the PMIA model has these properties. The greedy algorithm also achieves the $1 - 1/e$ approximation under a new propriety identified by Chen et al. called "sequence submodularity". The runtime has several order-of-magnitude improvement as well. It also outperforms centrality-based heuristics on large datasets (millions of edges) [5].

4.4.3   SIMPATH Algorithm

According to the hardness of influence spread under the LT model, Goyal et al. [4] leverage heuristic algorithm to tackle this problem. The key intuition behind SIMPATH algorithm is to enumerate the simple paths from the seed set instead of running costly simulations. A *simple path* is a directed path in a graph where no nodes are repeated. Let $\Upsilon_{u,v}$ be the probability that v is infected by u. If P_{uv} be the set of simple paths between u and v, then we have the following relationship:

$$\Upsilon_{u,v} = \sum_{P \in P_{uv}} Pr(P) \tag{4.9}$$

Where Pr is computed as: for some subset S, $\mathscr{X}$ of V, let $\sigma^S(\mathscr{X})$ be the expected number of infectees in the LT model given seed set $\mathscr{X}$ on the subgraph induced by the set of nodes in S. So, the expected number of infectees is:

$$\sigma(\mathscr{X}) = \sum_{u \in \mathscr{X}} \sigma^{V - \mathscr{X} + \{u\}}(u) \tag{4.10}$$

Algorithm 4 SIMPATH Spread Algorithm

1: **procedure** SIMPATHSPREAD($\mathcal{X}$)
2:     $\sigma = 0$
3:     **for** $u \in \mathcal{X}$ **do**
4:         Compute all simple paths from u to all other nodes in the graph $G(V - \mathcal{X} + u)$
5:         Compute the probability for all the paths, let this equal T
6:         $\sigma = \sigma + T$
7:     **end for**
8:     **return** σ
9: **end procedure**

According to the Eq. (4.9), the expected spread for a singleton is the sum of the probability of each node being influenced as follows:

$$\sigma(\{u\}) = \sum_{v \in V} \Upsilon_{u,v} \tag{4.11}$$

So, we can compute the expected number of infectees as follows:

$$\sigma(\mathcal{X}) = \sum_{u \in \mathcal{X}} \sum_{v \in V - \mathcal{X} + \{u\}} \sum_{P \in P_{uv} \text{ on } G(V - \mathcal{X} + u)} Pr(P) \tag{4.12}$$

Let us suppose we have an oracle that enumerates all simple paths from some node u to all other nodes within a graph. Goyal et al. use the backtrack algorithm to achieve this. We can compute σ exactly as Algorithm 4.

As we said, computing the expected number of infectees in the LT model is #P hard because just counting the number of simple paths between nodes is #P hard. So, Algorithm 4 is not efficient—as it computes σ exactly. As the longer paths will occur with a much lower probability (the influence events are independent), a heuristic is only enumerating the paths that have a probability greater than a certain threshold. Hence, SIMPATH computes a lower bound on the expected number of infectees—the hope is that the paths it does not consider, do not add up to a whole lot which, would make the lower bound tight. This is not an approximation guarantee— there are currently no known results regarding how close this bound is to the actual expected value. However, the threshold can be used to trade runtime for accuracy.

The overall algorithm for scalable influence maximization under the LT model is called SIMPATH and calls SIMPATH-Spread to approximate σ. Goyel et al. leverage lazy submodular evaluation as well as some graph-theoretic techniques to limit the calls to SIMPATH-Spread. However, one major issue is to limit the number of calls to SIMPATH-Spread on the first iteration of the greedy algorithm. SIMPATH shortens the runtime of the first iteration by computing SIMPATH Spread for nodes within a vertex cover.

SIMPATH performed comparable to the greedy algorithm and outperform degree centrality, PageRank, and LDAG [5] in terms of expected number of infectees and provides $3 - 4x$ order of magnitude improvement over the greedy in terms of runtime.

4.5   Conclusion

In this chapter we reviewed the popular independent cascade and linear threshold models as well as their associated influence maximization problems. We also described various algorithmic approaches to these problems and the current state-of-the-art techniques for achieving scalability. However, as with the tipping model and SIR model of the previous chapters, this framework does not take the attributes of the nodes and edges into account during the diffusion process. In the next chapter, we describe a logic-programming based framework that includes this dimension.

References

1. Kempe, David and Kleinberg, Jon and Tardos. Maximizing the spread of influence through a social network. (2003) ACM 137–146.
2. Nemhauser, George L and Wolsey, Laurence A and Fisher, Marshall L. An analysis of approximations for maximizing submodular set functions. (1978) 14(1) 265–294.
3. Mossel, Elchanan and Roch, Sebastien. On the submodularity of influence in social networks. (2007) ACM 128–134.
4. Goyal, Amit and Lu, Wei and Lakshmanan, Laks VS. Simpath: An efficient algorithm for influence maximization under the linear threshold model.(2011) Data Mining (ICDM), 2011 IEEE 11th International Conference, 211–220.
5. Chen, Wei and Wang, Chi and Wang, Yajun. Scalable influence maximization for prevalent viral marketing in large-scale social networks. (2010) Proceedings of the 16th ACM SIGKDD international conference on Knowledge discovery and data mining, 1029–1038.
6. Shakarian, Paulo and Salmento, Joseph and Pulleyblank, William and Bertetto, John. Reducing gang violence through network influence based targeting of social programs. (2014) 20th ACM SIGKDD international conference on Knowledge discovery and data mining, 1829–1836
7. Lu, Wei and Lakshmanan, Laks VS. Profit maximization over social networks. (2012) arXiv preprint arXiv:1210.4211
8. Minoux, Michel. Accelerated greedy algorithms for maximizing submodular set functions. (1978) , Optimization Techniques 234–243.
9. Wang, Chi and Chen, Wei and Wang, Yajun. Scalable influence maximization for independent cascade model in large-scale social networks (2012) Data Mining and Knowledge Discovery. 545–576.

Chapter 5
Logic Programming Based Diffusion Models

5.1 Introduction

This chapter focuses on a logic-programming approach to social network diffusion first introduced in [23] and later extended in [4]. The advantage with this approach is that we can not only consider the topology of the network, but also consider labeled attributes of the nodes and edges in a natural way. Since its introduction, there have been other variants of the logic-based approach that have leveraged formalisms such as PSL [2] and modal logic [24] in addition to tackling problems such as non-monotonic diffusion reasoning [25] and informing the creation of diffusion-specific centrality measures [26]. These approaches differ from some of the diffusion models in previous chapters in several key ways. For instance, the other models largely assume that a social network is nothing but a set of vertices and edges [16–18]. In contrast, in this chapter we adopt a richer model where edges and vertices can both be labeled with properties. For instance, a political campaigner hoping to spread a positive message about a campaign needs to use demographics (e.g. sex, age group, educational level, group affiliations, etc.) for targeting a political message—a "one size fits all" message will not work. In general, social network researchers would say that they have several sociomatrices that can be used for such applications. Another key difference is that the approaches of the previous chapters reason about a single diffusion model, rather than develop a framework for reasoning about a whole class of diffusion models.

Past diffusion models developed in a variety of fields ranging from business [10], economics [21], social science [20], epidemiology [15, 22, 27], mobile phone usage [11] show that diffusion models vary dramatically from application to application. In this chapter, we organize these models into three broad categories.

1. *Cascade models* [15, 22, 27] are widespread in epidemiology and assume that diffusions are largely based on connectivity between nodes and are largely probabilistic.

© The Author(s) 2015

P. Shakarian et al., *Diffusion in Social Networks*, SpringerBriefs
in Computer Science, DOI 10.1007/978-3-319-23105-1_5

2. *Tipping models* do not use probabilities, but use various quantitative calculations to determine when a vertex adopts (or is infected with) a diffusive property. They are omnipresent in the social sciences and business [7, 12, 20]. Nobel-laureate Tom Schelling makes a similar point that diffusions in many social science applications have a tipping point when vertices become influenced by the number of neighbors and the strength of commitment the neighbors may have to a certain position. No probabilities are present in such models.
3. *Homophilic models* are ones where similarity between users, rather than networks effects, dominate diffusion. Similarity is usually calculated using some quantitative model, often related to distance between vectors representing (values of) properties of nodes. For example, [11] tracks adoption of mobile applications in a study of over 27M users and shows that homophily—similarity between users—is the most compelling diffusion model. There are no probabilities here, just similarity measures. Another world famous diffusion model focused on marketing [10] also is based on homophily and similarity of nodes' intrinsic properties rather than a probability.

Moreover, many models use a mix of the above forms. For instance, Cha et al. [5] argues that the way photos are marked as "favorites" on Flickr is based on a mix of cascading and homophilic behavior and to study the former, one must also account for the latter. A similar combination of cascading and tipping is observed in [21]. In general, a language to express diffusion models must be capable of expressing a wide variety of *quantitative* methods encapsulated in the above.

In this chapter, we first show that a class of the well-known generalized annotated program (GAP) paradigm [6] form a convenient method to express many diffusion models. We focus on reasoning with diffusion models (expressed via GAPs) *after the diffusion models have been learned*. In particular, we consider the problem of optimal decision making in social networks which have associated diffusion models expressible as Linear GAPs, though many of the results in this chapter apply to arbitrary GAPs as well. Here are two examples.

- **(Q1) Cell Phone Plans** A cell phone company is promoting a new cell phone plan—as a promotion, it is giving away k free plans to existing customers.[1] Which set of k people should they pick so as to *maximize* the *number* of plan adoptees predicted by a cell phone plan adoption diffusion model they have learned from their past promotions?
- **(Q2) Medication Distribution Plan** A government combating a disease spread by physical contact has limited stocks of free medication to give away. Based on a diffusion model of how the disease spreads (e.g. kids might be more susceptible than adults, those previously inoculated against the disease are safe, etc.), they want to find a set of k people who (jointly) maximally spread the disease when

---

[1]This framework allows us to add additional constraints—for instance, that plans can only be given to customers satisfying certain conditions, e.g.customers deemed to be "good" according to various business criteria.

infected (so that they can provide immediate treatment to these k people in an attempt to halt the disease's spread).[2] Notice that this query corresponds to only one of many different policies that can be considered to deal with the disease spread scenario, that is, we consider the case where a diffusion model expressing how an infected person can infect other people is available and formulate a query that looks at the maximum spread when k people are infected. Other queries, possibly leading to different answers about who should be treated with medications, are possible.

Both these problems are instances of a class of queries that we call *Social Network Diffusion Optimization Problem* (SNDOP) queries. They differ from other queries studied in logic programming in two fundamental ways: (1) They are specialized to operate on graph data where the graph's vertices and edges are labeled with properties and where the edges can have associated weights, (2) They find *sets of vertices* that optimize complex objective functions that can be specified by the user.

This chapter is organized as follows. In Sect. 5.2, we provide an overview of GAPs (past work), define a social network (SN for short), and explain how GAPs can represent some types of diffusion in SNs. Section 5.3 formally defines different types of social network diffusion optimization problems and provides results on their computational complexity and other properties. Section 5.4 shows how our framework can represent several existing diffusion models for social networks including economics and epidemiology. In Sect. 5.5 we present the exact SNDOP-Mon algorithm to answer SNDOP queries under certain assumptions of monotonicity. We then develop a greedy algorithm GREEDY-SNDOP and show that under certain conditions, it is guaranteed to be an $\left(\frac{e}{e-1}\right)$ approximation algorithm for SNDOP queries—this is the best possible approximation guarantee. Last, but not least, we describe our prototype implementation and experiments in Sect. 5.5. Specifically, we tested our GREEDY-SNDOP algorithm on a real-world social network data set derived from Wikipedia logs. We show that we solve social network diffusion optimization problems over real data sets in acceptable times.

5.2 Embedding Diffusion Models into Annotated Logic Programs

In this section, we first formalize social networks, then briefly review generalized annotated logic programs (GAPs) [6] and then describe how GAPs can be used to represent concepts related to diffusion in social networks.

---

[2] Again, this framework allows us to add additional constraints—for instance, that medication can only be given to people satisfying certain conditions, e.g. be over a certain age, or be within a certain age range and not have any conditions that are contra-indicators for the medication in question.

5.2.1 Social Networks Formalization

Throughout this chapter, we assume the existence of two arbitrary but fixed disjoint sets VP, EP of *vertex* and *edge predicate symbols* respectively. Each vertex predicate symbol has arity 1 and each edge predicate symbol has arity 2.

Definition 5.1. A **social network** is a 5-tuple $(\mathbf{V}, \mathbf{E}, \ell_{vert}, \ell_{edge}, w)$ where:

1. $\mathbf{V}$ is a finite set whose elements are called *vertices*.
2. $\mathbf{E} \subseteq \mathbf{V} \times \mathbf{V}$ is a finite *multi-set* whose elements are called *edges*.
3. $\ell_{vert} : \mathbf{V} \rightarrow 2^{VP}$ is a function, called *vertex labeling function*.
4. $\ell_{edge} : \mathbf{E} \rightarrow EP$ is a function, called *edge labeling function*.[3]
5. $w : \mathbf{E} \rightarrow [0,1]$ is a function, called *weight function*.

We now present a brief example of an SN.

Example 5.1. Let us return to the cell phone example (query **(Q1)**). Figure 5.1 shows a toy social network the cell phone company might use. Here, we might have $VP = \{male, female, adopter, temp\_adopter, non\_adopter\}$ denoting the sex and past adoption behavior of each vertex; EP might be the set $\{phone, email, IM\}$ denoting the types of interactions between vertices (phone call, email, and instant messaging respectively). The function ℓ_{vert} is shown in Fig. 5.1 by the shape (denoting past adoption status) and shading (male/female). The type of edges (bold for phone, dashed for email, dotted for IM) is used to depict ℓ_{edge}. $w(\langle v_1, v_2 \rangle)$ denotes the percentage of communications of type $\ell_{edge}(\langle v_1, v_2 \rangle)$ initiated by v_1 that were with v_2 (measured either w.r.t. time or bytes).

It is important to note that our definition of social networks is much broader than that used by several researchers [10, 11, 22, 27] who often do not consider either ℓ_{edge} or ℓ_{vert} or edge weights through the function w—it is well-known in marketing that intrinsic properties of vertices (customers, patients) and the nature and strength of the relationships (edges) is critical for decision making in those fields.

Note We assume that SNs satisfy various integrity constraints. In Example 5.1, it is clear that $\ell_{vert}(v)$ should include at most one of *male,female* and at most one of *adopter, temp_adopter,non_adopter*. *We assume the existence of some integrity constraints to ensure this kind of semantic integrity*—they can be written in any reasonable syntax to express ICs—in the rest of this chapter, we assume that social networks have associated ICs and that they satisfy them. In our example, we will assume ICs ensuring that a vertex can be marked with at most one of *male,female* and at most one of *adopter, temp_adopter, non_adopter*.

---

[3]Each edge $e \in \mathbf{E}$ is labeled by exactly one predicate symbol from EP. However, there can be multiple edges between two vertices labeled with different predicate symbols.

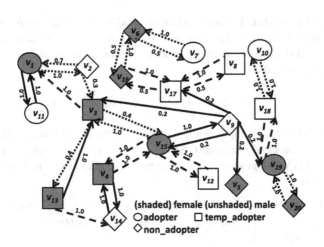

Fig. 5.1 Example cellular network

5.2.2 Generalized Annotated Programs: A Recap

We now recapitulate the definition of generalized annotated logic programs from [6]. We assume the existence of a set AVar of variable symbols ranging over the unit real interval $[0,1]$ and a set $\mathscr{F}$ of function symbols each of which has an associated arity. We start by defining annotations.

Definition 5.2 (Annotation). Annotations are inductively defined as follows:

(i) Any member of $[0,1] \cup$ AVar is an annotation.
(ii) If $f \in \mathscr{F}$ is an n-ary function symbol and $t_1, \ldots, t_n$ are annotations, then $f(t_1, \ldots, t_n)$ is an annotation.

For instance, $0.5, 1, 0.3$ and X are all annotations (here X is assumed to be a variable in AVar). If $+, *, /$ are all binary function symbols in $\mathscr{F}$, then $\frac{(X+1)*0.5}{0.3}$ is an annotation.[4]

We define a separate logical language whose constants are members of **V** and whose predicate symbols consist of VP $\cup$ EP. We also assume the existence of a set $\mathscr{V}$ of variable symbols ranging over the constants (vertices). No function symbols are present. Terms and atoms are defined in the usual way (cf. [19]). If $A = p(t_1, \ldots, t_n)$ is an atom and $p \in$ VP (resp. $p \in$ EP), then A is called a *vertex* (resp. *edge*) atom. We will use $\mathscr{A}$ to denote the set of all ground atoms (i.e., atoms where no variable occurs).

---

[4]Notice that in [6] annotations are not restricted to be in $[0,1]$ but any upper semi-lattice is allowed—for the purpose of this chapter we will restrict ourselves to the unit real interval.

Definition 5.3 (Annotated Atom/GAP-Rule/GAP). If A is an atom and μ is an annotation, then $A : \mu$ is an *annotated atom*. If A is a vertex (resp. edge) atom, then $A : \mu$ is also called *vertex* (resp. *edge*) annotated atom. If $A_0 : \mu_0, A_1 : \mu_1, \ldots, A_n : \mu_n$ are annotated atoms, then

$$A_0 : \mu_0 \leftarrow A_1 : \mu_1 \wedge \ldots \wedge A_n : \mu_n$$

is called a *GAP rule* (or simply *rule*). When $n = 0$, the above rule is called a *fact*.[5] A *generalized annotated program* (GAP) is a finite set of rules. An annotated atom (resp. a rule, a GAP) is *ground* iff there are no occurrences of variables from either AVar or $\mathscr{V}$ in it.

Every social network $\mathscr{S} = (\mathbf{V}, \mathbf{E}, \ell_{vert}, \ell_{edge}, w)$ can be represented by the GAP $\Pi_{\mathscr{S}} = \{q(v) : 1 \leftarrow \mid v \in \mathbf{V} \wedge q \in \ell_{vert}(v)\} \cup \{ep(v_1, v_2) : w(\langle v_1, v_2 \rangle) \leftarrow \mid \langle v_1, v_2 \rangle \in \mathbf{E} \wedge \ell_{edge}(\langle v_1, v_2 \rangle) = ep\}$.

Definition 5.4 (Embedded Social Network). A social network $\mathscr{S}$ is said to be *embedded* in a GAP Π iff $\Pi_{\mathscr{S}} \subseteq \Pi$.

It is clear that all social networks can be represented as GAPs. When we augment $\Pi_{\mathscr{S}}$ with other rules—such as rules describing how certain properties diffuse through the social network, we get a GAP $\Pi \supseteq \Pi_{\mathscr{S}}$ that captures both the structure of the SN and the diffusion principles. Here is a small example of such a GAP.

Example 5.2. The GAP Π_{cell} might consist of $\Pi_{\mathscr{S}}$ using the social network of Fig. 5.1 plus the GAP-rules:

1. $will\_adopt(V_0) : 0.8 \times X + 0.2 \leftarrow adopter(V_0) : 1 \wedge male(V_0) : 1 \wedge$
   $IM(V_0, V_1) : 0.3 \wedge female(V_1) : 1 \wedge will\_adopt(V_1) : X.$
2. $will\_adopt(V_0) : 0.9 \times X + 0.1 \leftarrow adopter(V_0) : 1 \wedge male(V_0) : 1 \wedge$
   $IM(V_0, V_1) : 0.3 \wedge male(V_1) : 1 \wedge will\_adopt(V_1) : X.$
3. $will\_adopt(V_0) : 1 \leftarrow temp\_adopter(V_0) :$
   $1 \wedge male(V_0) : 1 \wedge email(V_1, V_0) : 1 \wedge female(V_1) : 1 \wedge will\_adopt(V_1) : 1.$

Rule (1) says that if V_0 is a male adopter and V_1 is female and the weight of V_0's instant messages to V_1 is 0.3 or more, and we previously thought that V_1 would be an adopter with confidence X, then we can infer that V_0 will adopt the new plan with confidence $0.8 \times X + 0.2$. The other rules may be similarly read.

Suppose $\mathscr{S}$ is a social network and $\Pi \supseteq \Pi_{\mathscr{S}}$ is a GAP. In this case, we call the rules in $\Pi - \Pi_{\mathscr{S}}$ *diffusion rules*. In this chapter we consider a restricted class of GAPs: every rule with a non-empty body has a vertex annotated atom in the head ([6] allows any atom to appear in the head of a rule). Thus, edge atoms can appear only in rule bodies or facts. This means that neither edge weights nor edge labels change as the result of the diffusion. However, for the general case, it is possible for them to change as a result of the diffusion process.

---

[5]For notational simplicity, we will often write a fact $A_0 : \mu_0 \leftarrow$ simply as $A_0 : \mu_0$, i.e. we drop the symbol $\leftarrow$.

GAPs have a formal semantics that can be immediately used. An interpretation I is any mapping from the set $\mathscr{A}$ of all grounds atoms to $[0,1]$. The set $\mathscr{I}$ of all interpretations can be partially ordered via the ordering: $I_1 \preceq I_2$ iff for all ground atoms A, $I_1(A) \leq I_2(A)$. $\mathscr{I}$ forms a complete lattice under the $\preceq$ ordering.

Definition 5.5 (Satisfaction/Entailment). An interpretation I *satisfies* a ground annotated atom $A : \mu$, denoted $I \models A : \mu$, iff $I(A) \geq \mu$. I satisfies a ground GAP-rule r of the form $AA_0 \leftarrow AA_1 \wedge \ldots \wedge AA_n$ (denoted $I \models r$) iff either (i) I satisfies AA_0 or (ii) there exists an $1 \leq i \leq n$ such that I does not satisfy AA_i. I *satisfies* a non-ground annotated atom (rule) iff I satisfies all ground instances of it. I *satisfies* a GAP iff I satisfies all rules in it. A GAP Π *entails* an annotated atom AA, denoted $\Pi \models AA$, iff every interpretation I that satisfies Π also satisfies AA.

As shown by Kifer and Subrahmanian [6], we can associate a fixpoint operator with any GAP Π that maps interpretations to interpretations.

Definition 5.6. Suppose Π is any GAP and I an interpretation. The mapping $\mathbf{T}_\Pi$ that maps interpretations to interpretations is defined as $\mathbf{T}_\Pi(I)(A) = \sup\{\mu \,|\, A : \mu \leftarrow AA_1 \wedge \ldots \wedge AA_n$ is a ground instance of a rule in Π and for all $1 \leq i \leq n$, $I \models AA_i\}$.

The results of [6] show that $\mathbf{T}_\Pi$ is monotonic (w.r.t. $\preceq$) and has a least fixpoint $lfp(\mathbf{T}_\Pi)$. Moreover, they show that Π entails $A : \mu$ iff $\mu \leq lfp(\mathbf{T}_\Pi)(A)$ and hence $lfp(\mathbf{T}_\Pi)$ precisely captures the ground atomic logical consequences of Π. They also define the *iteration* of $\mathbf{T}_\Pi$ as follows: $\mathbf{T}_\Pi \uparrow 0$ is the interpretation that assigns 0 to all ground atoms; $\mathbf{T}_\Pi \uparrow (i+1) = \mathbf{T}_\Pi(\mathbf{T}_\Pi \uparrow i)$.

The semantics of GAPs requires that when there are multiple ground instances of GAP-rules with the same head that "fire", the highest annotation in any of these ground rules is "chosen" according to the semantics of GAPs. This might seem restrictive and counter-intuitive to some, but it actually is the source of much power of GAPs. For instance, one school of thought is that when multiple ground rules with the same head "fire", the annotation derived should be the "noisy-or" value derived by combining the values of the annotations in the heads of firing rules. However, this is just one way of combining evidence from multiple sources many other triangular co-norms other than noisy-or can be used and have been used in the literature. However, such T-norms can be expressed in our framework. If we have ground rules $G_1, G_2, \ldots, G_n$, each having the same atom in the head, and we want to combine evidence using a triangular co-norm[6] $\oplus$, and if G_i has the form:

$$A : \mu_i \leftarrow Body_i$$

then we can replace these rules with the rules:

$$A : \oplus(\{\mu_i \,|\, i \in X\}) \leftarrow \bigwedge_{i \in X} Body_i$$

---

[6]When we apply $\oplus$ to a set $\{x_1, \ldots, x_k\}$, we use $\oplus(\{x_1, \ldots, x_k\})$ as short-hand for $\oplus(x_1, \oplus(\{x_2, \ldots, x_n\}))$ which is well defined as all triangular co-norms are commutative and associative.

for any subset $X \subseteq \{1,\ldots,n\}$. Moreover, as we have already remarked, many real-world diffusion models are non-probabilistic, making assumptions about how annotations should be combined harder to justify. However, the above discussion shows that the GAP framework is capable of expressing such rules. Though there is clearly a cost in terms of difficulty of expressing such methods to combine evidence generated by multiple rules, algorithms already exist and have been implemented [2] to learn GAP-based diffusion rules automatically from social network time series data.

We will show (in Sect. 5.4) that many existing diffusion models for a variety of phenomena can be expressed as a GAP $\Pi \supseteq \Pi_{\mathscr{S}}$ by adding some GAP-rules describing the diffusion process to $\Pi_{\mathscr{S}}$.

5.3 Social Network Diffusion Optimization Problem (SNDOP) Queries

5.3.1 Basic SNDOP Queries

In this section, we develop a formal syntax and semantics for optimization in social networks, taking advantage of the aforementioned embedding of SNs into GAPs. In particular, we formally define SNDOP queries, examples of which have been informally introduced earlier as (**Q1**) and (**Q2**). We see from queries (**Q1**) and (**Q2**) that a SNDOP query looks for a **set V′** of vertices and has the following components: (1) an objective function expressed via an aggregate operator, (2) an integer $k > 0$, (3) a set of conditions that each vertex in **V′** must satisfy, (4) an "input" atom $g_I(V)$, and (v) an "output" atom $g_O(V)$ (here g_I and g_O are vertex predicate symbols, whereas V is a variable).

Aggregates It is clear that in order to express queries like (**Q1**) and (**Q2**), we need aggregate operators which are mappings $agg : \mathsf{FM}([0,1]) \to \mathbb{R}^+$ ($\mathbb{R}^+$ is the set of non-negative reals) where $\mathsf{FM}(X)$ denotes the set of all finite multisets that are subsets of X. Relational DB aggregates like SUM,COUNT,AVG,MIN,MAX are all aggregate operators which can take a finite multiset of non-negative reals as input and return a single non-negative real.

Vertex Condition A vertex condition is a set of vertex annotated atoms containing exactly one variable (intuitively, such annotated atoms are conditions that must be jointly satisfied by a vertex). More formally, a vertex condition VC is a set $\{p_1(V) : \mu_1,\ldots,p_n(V) : \mu_n\}$ where each $p_i \in \mathsf{VP}$, $V \in \mathscr{V}$, and each $\mu_i \in [0,1]$. We use $VC[V/v]$ to denote the set of ground annotated atoms obtained from VC by replacing each occurrence of V with v, that is $VC[V/v] = \{p_1(v) : \mu_1,\ldots,p_n(v) : \mu_n\}$. A GAP Π entails $VC[V/v]$, denoted $\Pi \models VC[V/v]$, iff $\Pi \models p_i(v) : \mu_i$ for all $1 \leq i \leq n$.

Thus, in our example, $\{male(V) : 1, adopter(V) : 1\}$ is a vertex condition, but $\{male(V) : 1, email(V,V') : 1\}$ is not. We are now ready to define a SNDOP query.

Definition 5.7 (SNDOP Query). A *SNDOP query* is a 5-tuple $(agg, VC, k, g_I(V), g_O(V))$ where *agg* is an aggregate, *VC* is a vertex condition, $k > 0$ is an integer, and $g_I(V), g_O(V)$ are vertex atoms.

Let us consider again the medication distribution plan example. Suppose we have a diffusion model expressing how a property *healthy* diffuses in a social network w.r.t. a property *immune* (which would hold for a vertex when a medication is given to it). An interesting query to pose would be to determine a set of at most k people such that if these people were immune to the disease, then the number of healthy people would be maximized. Such a query can be expressed with the SNDOP query $(\text{SUM}, \emptyset, k, immune(V), healthy(V))$. Here, the goal is to find a set $\mathbf{V'} \subseteq \mathbf{V}$ of vertices such that $|\mathbf{V'}| \leq k$ and the following is maximized:

$$\text{SUM}\{lfp(\mathbf{T}_{\Pi \cup \{immune(v'):1 \,|\, v' \in \mathbf{V'}\}})(healthy(v)) \,|\, v \in \mathbf{V}\}$$

Here, the SUM is applied to a multiset rather than a set. Note that in the query above $VC = \emptyset$, meaning that the *immune* property can be assigned to any vertex of the SN. However, other queries can be expressed where *VC* imposes restrictions on which vertices can have property *immune*. As an example, $VC = \{adult(V)\}$ would enforce every vertex in $\mathbf{V'}$ to be an adult person.

If we return to our cell phone example, we can set $agg = \text{SUM}$, $VC = \emptyset$, $k = 3$ (for example), $g_I(V) = will\_adopt(V)$, and $g_O(V) = will\_adopt(V)$ (notice that in this case $g_I(V) = g_O(V)$). Here also, the goal is to find a set $\mathbf{V'} \subseteq \mathbf{V}$ of vertices such that $|\mathbf{V'}| \leq 3$ and the following is maximized:

$$\text{SUM}\{lfp(\mathbf{T}_{\Pi \cup \{will\_adopt(v'):1 \,|\, v' \in \mathbf{V'}\}})(will\_adopt(v)) \,|\, v \in \mathbf{V}\}$$

Here, the SUM is applied to a multiset rather than a set. Note that the diffusion model's impact is captured via the $lfp(\mathbf{T}_{\Pi \cup \{will\_adopt(v'):1 \,|\, v' \in \mathbf{V'}\}})(will\_adopt(v))$ expression which, intuitively, tells us the confidence (according to the diffusion model) that each vertex v will be an adopter. If we return to an extended version of our cell phone example and we want to ensure that the vertices in $\mathbf{V'}$ are "good" customers[7] then we merely can set $VC = \{good(V) : 1\}$. This query now asks us to find a set $\mathbf{V'}$ of three or less vertices—all of which are "good" customers of the company C—such that $\text{SUM}\{lfp(\mathbf{T}_{\Pi \cup \{will\_adopt(v'):1 \,|\, v' \in \mathbf{V'}\}})(will\_adopt(v)) \,|\, v \in \mathbf{V}\}$ is maximized.

Our framework also allows the vertex condition *VC* to have annotations other than 1. So in our cell phone example, the company could explicitly exclude anyone whose "opinion" toward the company is negative. If opinion is quantified on a continuous $[0, 1]$ scale (such automated systems do exist [1]), then the vertex condition might be restated as $VC = \{good(V) : 1, negative\_opinion\_C(V) : 0.7\}$

---

[7]We can think of many ways a company may define "good" customers, e.g. those who regularly pay their bills on time, those who buy a lot of services from the company, those who have stayed as customers for a long time, etc. For our example, the specific definition of "good" is not relevant.

which says that the company wants to exclude anyone whose negativity about the company exceeds 0.7 according to an opinion scoring engine such as [1].

Definition 5.8 (Pre-answer/Value). Consider a social network $\mathscr{S} = (\mathbf{V}, \mathbf{E}, \ell_{vert}, \ell_{edge}, w)$ embedded in a GAP Π. A *pre-answer* to the SNDOP query $Q = (agg, VC, k, g_I(V), g_O(V))$ w.r.t. Π is any set $\mathbf{V}' \subseteq \mathbf{V}$ such that:

1. $|\mathbf{V}'| \leq k$, and
2. for all vertices $v'' \in \mathbf{V}'$, $\Pi \cup \{g_I(v') : 1 \mid v' \in \mathbf{V}'\} \models VC[V/v'']$.

We use pre_ans(Q, Π) to denote the set of all pre-answers to Q w.r.t. Π (whenever Π is clear from the context we simply write pre_ans(Q)).

The *value* of a pre-answer $\mathbf{V}'$ is defined as follows:

$$value(\mathbf{V}') = agg(\{lfp(\mathbf{T}_{\Pi \cup \{g_I(v'):1 \mid v' \in \mathbf{V}'\}})(g_O(v)) \mid v \in \mathbf{V}\})$$

where the aggregate is applied to a multi-set rather than a set. We also note that we can define *value* as a mapping from interpretations to reals based on a SNDOP query. We say $value(I) = agg(\{I(g_O(v)) \mid v \in \mathbf{V}\})$.

If we return to our cell phone example, $\mathbf{V}'$ is the set of vertices to which the company is considering giving free plans. $value(\mathbf{V}')$ is computed as follows.

1. Find the least fixpoint of $\mathbf{T}_{\Pi'_{cell}}$ where Π'_{cell} is Π_{cell} expanded with facts of the form $will\_adopt(v') : 1$ for each vertex $v' \in \mathbf{V}'$.
2. For each vertex $v \in \mathbf{V}$ (the entire set of vertices, not just $\mathbf{V}'$ now), we now find the confidence assigned by the least fixpoint.
3. Summing up these confidences gives us a measure of the expected number of plan adoptees.

Definition 5.9 (Answer). Suppose a social network $\mathscr{S} = (\mathbf{V}, \mathbf{E}, \ell_{vert}, \ell_{edge}, w)$ is embedded in a GAP Π and $Q = (agg, VC, k, g_I(V), g_O(V))$ is a SNDOP query. A pre-answer $\mathbf{V}'$ is an *answer* to the SNDOP query Q w.r.t. Π iff the SNDOP query has no other pre-answer $\mathbf{V}''$ such that $value(\mathbf{V}'') > value(\mathbf{V}')$.[8]

The *answer set* to SNDOP query Q w.r.t. Π, denoted ans(Q, Π), is the set of all answers to Q w.r.t. Π (whenever Π is clear from the context we simply write ans(Q)).

It is important to note that an answer to an SNDOP query is a **set** of vertices that **jointly** maximize the objective function specified. Thus, it is entirely possible that if we set $k = 1$, we could have two answers $\{a_1\}$ and $\{a_2\}$ each of which ties for the highest value. However, $\{a_1, a_2\}$ may *not* be the answer that optimizes the objective function when $k = 2$.

---

[8]Throughout this chapter, we only treat maximization problems—there is no loss of generality in this because minimizing an objective function f is the same as maximizing $-f$.

Example 5.3. For instance, suppose a_1 and a_2 are brothers with largely the same connections. The sets $\{a_1\}$ and $\{a_2\}$ both have value 100 each and let us say these constitute an answer (looking at one individual only) w.r.t. an objective function, e.g. influencing voters in an election to vote for candidate X. As a_1, a_2 mostly influence the same people, they may jointly be able to get only 110 people to vote for the candidate because of the large overlap in their sphere of influence. However, now consider persons a_3, a_4. Each of them can only influence 90 voters by themselves, but only 10 of these voters "overlap". Thus, they can jointly influence $80 + 80 + 10 = 170$ voters to vote for X. It would make more sense (all other things being equal) for the candidate's party to invest in $\{a_3, a_4\}$.

Example 5.4. Consider the GAP Π_{cell} of Example 5.2 with the social network from Fig. 5.1 embedded and the SNDOP query $Q_{cell} = (SUM, \emptyset, 3, will\_adopt, will\_adopt)$. The sets $\mathbf{V}_1' = \{v_{15}, v_{19}, v_6\}$ and $\mathbf{V}_2' = \{v_{15}, v_{18}, v_6\}$ are both *pre-answers*. In the case of $\mathbf{V}_1'$, two applications of the $\mathbf{T}_\Pi$ operator yields a fixpoint where the vertex atoms formed with *will_adopt* and vertices in the set $\{v_{15}, v_{19}, v_6, v_{12}, v_{18}, v_7, v_{10}\}$ are annotated with 1. For $\mathbf{V}_2$, only one application of $\mathbf{T}_\Pi$ is required to reach a fixpoint. In the fixpoint, vertex atoms formed with *will_adopt* and vertices in the set $\{v_{15}, v_6, v_{12}, v_{18}, v_7, v_{10}\}$ are annotated with 1. As these are the only vertex atoms formed with *will_adopt* that have a non-zero annotation after reaching the fixed point, we know that $value(\mathbf{V}_1') = 7$ and $value(\mathbf{V}_2') = 6$.

5.3.2   Special Cases of SNDOPs

In this section, we examine several special cases of SNDOPs that still allow us to represent a wide variety of diffusion models. Table 5.1 illustrates the special cases discussed in this section while Table 5.2 illustrates various properties we prove (and the assumptions under which those properties are proved).

Special Cases of GAPs First, we present a class of GAPs called *linear* GAPs. Intuitively, a GAP is linear if the annotations in the rule heads are linear functions and the annotations in the body are variables. It is important to note that a wide variety of diffusion models can be represented with GAPs that meet the requirements of this special case. We formally define linear GAPs below.

Table 5.1 Special cases of SNDOPs

Type	Special case	Reference
Special cases of Π	Linear GAP	Definition 5.10
Special cases of *agg*	Monotonic	Definition 5.11
	Positive-linear	Definition 5.12
Special cases of *value*	Normalized	Definition 5.13
	A-priori VC	Definition 5.14

Table 5.2 Properties that can be proven given certain assumptions

Property	Assumptions
Monotonicity of *value* (Lemma 5.1)	Monotonicity of *agg*
Multiset $\{V' \subseteq V \mid V'$ *is a pre-answer*$\}$ is a uniform matroid (Lemma 5.2)	A-priori VC
	Linear GAP
Submodularity of *value* (Theorem 5.1)	Positive-linear *agg*
	A-priori VC

Definition 5.10 (Linear GAP). A GAP-rule is *linear* iff it is of the form:

$$H_0 : c_0 + c_1 \cdot X_1 + \cdots + c_n \cdot X_n \leftarrow A_1 : X_1 \wedge \ldots \wedge A_n : X_n$$

where each $c_i \in [0,1]$, $\Sigma_{i=1}^{n} c_i \in [0,1]$, and each X_j is a variable in AVar. A GAP is linear iff each rule in it is linear.

Special Aggregates We define two types of aggregates: *monotonic* aggregates and *positive-linear* aggregates.

To define monotonicity, we first define a partial order $\sqsubseteq$ on multi-sets of numbers as follows: given two multi-sets of numbers X_1 and X_2, we write $X_1 \sqsubseteq X_2$ iff there exists an *injective* mapping $\beta : X_1 \rightarrow X_2$ such that $\forall x_1 \in X_1, x_1 \leq \beta(x_1)$.

Definition 5.11 (Monotonic Aggregate). An aggregate *agg* is **monotonic** iff whenever $X_1 \sqsubseteq X_2$, it is the case that $agg(X_1) \leq agg(X_2)$.

Definition 5.12 (Positive-Linear Aggregate). An aggregate *agg* is **positive-linear** iff it is defined as follows: $agg(X) = c_0 + \Sigma_{x_i \in X} c_i \cdot x_i$, where X is a finite multiset and $c_i \geq 0$ for all $i > 0$.

In the previous definition, note that c_0 can be positive, negative, or 0. Thus, we only require that the coefficients associated with the elements of the multi-set be positive—we allow for an additive constant to be negative. One obvious example of a positive-linear aggregate is SUM. Moreover, any positive weighted sum will also meet these requirements.

Proposition 5.1. *If agg is a positive-linear aggregate, then it is a monotonic aggregate.*

Special Cases of the Query We now describe two special cases of the query: *Normalized* and *a-priori VC* SNDOP queries. Intuitively, normalized means that $value(\emptyset) = 0$.

Definition 5.13 (Normalized). An SNDOP query is **Normalized** w.r.t. a given social network $\mathscr{S}$ and a GAP $\Pi \supseteq \Pi_{\mathscr{S}}$ iff $value(\emptyset) = 0$.

Note that the function *value* is *uniquely defined* by a social network, a SNDOP query, and a diffusion model Π and hence the above definition is well defined.

The following result states that if an SNDOP query Q with a positive-linear aggregate is not normalized, then we can always modify it into an "equivalent" SNDOP query Q' (i.e. $\text{ans}(Q) = \text{ans}(Q')$) which is normalized and still maintains a positive-linear aggregate.

Proposition 5.2. *Let* $Q = (agg, VC, k, g_I(V), g_O(V))$ *be a SNDOP query which is not normalized w.r.t. a social network* $\mathscr{S}$ *and a GAP* $\Pi \supseteq \Pi_{\mathscr{S}}$, *and where agg is positive-linear. Let* $agg'(X) = agg(X) - value(\emptyset)$. *Then,* $Q' = (agg', VC, k, g_I(V), g_O(V))$ *is a SNDOP query which is normalized w.r.t.* $\mathscr{S}$ *and* Π, $\text{ans}(Q) = \text{ans}(Q')$, *and agg' is positive-linear.*

Recall that in order to check if a set of vertices $\mathbf{V}'$ is a pre-answer, we need to check for all vertices $v'' \in \mathbf{V}'$ if $\Pi \cup \{g_I(v') : 1 \mid v' \in \mathbf{V}'\} \models VC[V/v'']$ (see condition (2) of Definition 5.8). Intuitively, a SNDOP query has an *A-Priori VC* (w.r.t. a given social network $\mathscr{S}$ and a GAP $\Pi \supseteq \Pi_{\mathscr{S}}$) when we can check this condition by looking only at the original social network $\mathscr{S}$ (thereby disregarding Π), that is we can check for all vertices $v'' \in \mathbf{V}'$ if $\Pi_{\mathscr{S}} \cup \{g_I(v'') : 1\} \models VC[V/v'']$. We formally define this notion below.

Definition 5.14 (A-Priori VC). A SNDOP query $Q = (agg, VC, k, g_I(V), g_O(V))$ has an **A-Priori VC** w.r.t. a given social network $\mathscr{S} = (\mathbf{V}, \mathbf{E}, \ell_{vert}, \ell_{edge}, w)$ and a GAP $\Pi \supseteq \Pi_{\mathscr{S}}$ iff for each $\mathbf{V}' \subseteq \mathbf{V}$ the following holds: for each $v'' \in \mathbf{V}'$, $\Pi \cup \{g_I(v') : 1 \mid v' \in \mathbf{V}'\} \models VC[V/v'']$ iff $\Pi_{\mathscr{S}} \cup \{g_I(v'') : 1\} \models VC[V/v'']$.

If, in the cell phone example, we require that the free cell phones are given to "good" vertices, then query **(Q1)** is a-priori VC because being "good" may be defined statically and is not determined by the diffusion process. Likewise, if we consider our medical example, in the case of an a-priori VC query **(Q2)** saying that an individual below 5 should not get the medicine, this boils down to a static labeling of each node's age (below 5 or not) which is not affected by the diffusion process. Table 5.2 summarizes the different properties that we prove in this section (as well as what assumptions we make to prove these properties).

We say that function *value* is monotonic iff $\mathbf{V}_1 \subseteq \mathbf{V}_2$ implies $value(\mathbf{V}_1) \leq value(\mathbf{V}_2)$ for any two sets of vertices $\mathbf{V}_1$ and $\mathbf{V}_2$. The first property we show is that the value function is monotonic if *agg* is monotonic.

Lemma 5.1. *Given a SNDOP query* $Q = (agg, VC, k, g_I(V), g_O(V))$, *a social network* $\mathscr{S}$, *and a GAP* $\Pi \supseteq \Pi_{\mathscr{S}}$, *if agg is monotonic (Definition 5.11), then value (defined as per Q and Π) is monotonic.*

Before introducing the next result we recall the definitions of matroid and uniform matroid. A *matroid* is a pair (X, I) where X is a finite set and I is a collection of subsets of X (called "independent"), satisfying two axioms:

1. $B \in I, A \subset B \Rightarrow A \in I$.
2. $A, B \in I, |A| < |B| \Rightarrow \exists x \in B - A \text{ s.t. } A \cup \{x\} \in I$.

A *uniform* matroid is a matroid such that independent sets are all sets of size at most k for some $k \geq 1$.

Next, we show that the set of pre-answers is a uniform matroid in the special case of an a-priori VC query.

Lemma 5.2. *Given a SNDOP query* $Q = (agg, VC, k, g_I(V), g_O(V))$, *a social network* $\mathscr{S}$, *and a GAP* $\Pi \supseteq \Pi_{\mathscr{S}}$, *if* Q *is a-priori VC w.r.t.* $\mathscr{S}$ *and* Π, *then the set of pre-answers is a uniform matroid.*

As we will see in Sect. 5.5, the above lemma (along with other properties, see Theorem 5.5) enables us to define a greedy approximation algorithm to solve SNDOP queries that achieves the best possible approximation ratio that a polynomial algorithm can achieve (unless **P** = **NP**).

An important property in social networks is *submodularity* whose relationship to the spread of phenomena in social networks has been extensively studied (see Chap. 4). If X is a set, then a function $f : 2^X \rightarrow \mathbb{R}$ is *submodular* iff whenever $X_1 \subseteq X_2 \subseteq X$ and $x \in X - X_2, f(X_1 \cup \{x\}) - f(X_1) \geq f(X_2 \cup \{x\}) - f(X_2)$. The following result states that the *value* function associated with a linear GAP and an a-priori VC SNDOP query whose aggregate is positive-linear is guaranteed to be submodular.

Theorem 5.1. *Given an SNDOP query* $Q = (agg, VC, k, g_I(V), g_O(V))$, *a social network* $\mathscr{S}$, *and a GAP* $\Pi \supseteq \Pi_{\mathscr{S}}$, *if the following criteria are met:*

- Π *is a linear GAP,*
- Q *is a-priori VC, and*
- *agg is positive-linear,*

then value (defined as per Q *and* Π *) is* **sub-modular***.*

5.3.3   The Complexity of SNDOP Queries

We now study the complexity of answering an SNDOP query. First, we show that SNDOP query answering is NP-hard by a reduction from max k-cover [14]. We show that the problem is NP-hard even when many of the special cases hold.

Theorem 5.2. *Finding an answer to an SNDOP query* $Q = (agg, VC, k, g_I(V), g_O(V))$ *(w.r.t. a social network* $\mathscr{S}$ *and a GAP* $\Pi \supseteq \Pi_{\mathscr{S}}$ *) is NP-hard (even if* Π *is a linear GAP, VC* $= \emptyset$, *agg* $= SUM$ *and value is normalized).*

Under some conditions, the decision problem for SNDOP queries is also in NP.

Theorem 5.3. *Given a SNDOP query* $Q = (agg, VC, k, g_I(V), g_O(V))$, *a social network* $\mathscr{S}$, *a GAP* $\Pi \supseteq \Pi_{\mathscr{S}}$, *and a real number target, the problem of checking whether there exists a pre-answer* $\mathbf{V}$ *s.t. value($\mathbf{V}$)* $\geq$ *target is in NP under the assumptions that agg and the functions in* $\mathscr{F}$ *are polynomially computable, and* Π *is ground.*

Most common aggregate functions like SUM, AVERAGE, Weighted average, MIN, MAX, COUNT are all polynomially computable. Moreover, the assumption that the functions corresponding to the function symbols in $\mathscr{F}$ (i.e. the function symbols that can appear in the annotations of a GAP) are polynomially computable is also reasonable.

Later in this chapter, we shall address the problem of answering a SNDOP query using an approximation algorithm. We say that $\mathbf{V}'$ is a $\frac{1}{\alpha}$-approximation to an SNDOP query if $value(\mathbf{V}_{opt}) \leq \alpha \cdot value(\mathbf{V}')$ (where $\mathbf{V}_{opt}$ is an answer to the SNDOP query). Likewise, the algorithm that produces $\mathbf{V}'$ in this case is an α-approximation algorithm. We note that due to the nature of the reduction from MAX-K-COVER that we used to prove NP-hardness, we can now show that unless $\mathbf{P} = \mathbf{NP}$, there is no PTIME-approximation of the SNDOP query answering problem that can guarantee that the approximate answer is better than 0.63 of the optimal value. This gives us an idea of the limits of approximation possible for a SNDOP query with a polynomial-time algorithm. Later, we will develop a greedy algorithm that precisely matches this approximation ratio.

Theorem 5.4. *Answering a SNDOP query $Q = (agg, VC, k, g_I(V), g_O(V))$ (w.r.t. a social network $\mathscr{S}$ and a GAP $\Pi \supseteq \Pi_{\mathscr{S}}$) cannot be approximated in PTIME within a ratio of $\frac{e-1}{e} + \varepsilon$ for some $\varepsilon > 0$ (where e is the inverse of the natural log) unless $\mathbf{P} = \mathbf{NP}$—even if Π is a linear GAP, $VC = \emptyset$, $agg = SUM$ and value is normalized.*

In other words, the previous theorem says that there is no polynomial-time algorithm that can approximate *value* within a factor of about 0.63 under standard assumptions.

5.4 Applying SNDOPs to Diffusion Problems

In this section, we show how SNDOPs can be applied to real-word diffusion problems. Most diffusion models in the literature fall into one of three categories— **tipping** models (Sect. 5.4.1), where a given vertex adopts a behavior based on the ratio of how many of its neighbors previously adopted the behavior, **cascade** models (Sect. 5.4.2), where a property passes from vertex to vertex solely based on the strength of the relationship between the vertices, and **homophilic** models (Sect. 5.4.3), where vertices with similar properties tend to adopt the same behavior—irrespective (or in addition to) of network relationships.

5.4.1 Tipping Diffusion

Tipping models [6, 20, 21] have been studied extensively in economics and sociology to understand diffusion phenomena. In tipping models, a vertex changes a property based on the cumulative effect of its neighbors. In this section, we present the tipping model of Jackon and Yariv [10], which generalizes many existing tipping models.

The Jackson-Yariv Diffusion Model [10] In this framework, the social network is just an undirected graph $\mathbf{G}' = (\mathbf{V}', \mathbf{E}')$ consisting of a set of agents (e.g. people). Each agent has a default behavior (A) and a new behavior (B). Suppose d_i denotes the degree of a vertex v_i. Jackson and Yariv [10] use a function $\gamma : \{0, \ldots, |\mathbf{V}'| - 1\} \rightarrow [0, 1]$ to describe how the number of neighbors of v affects the benefits to v for adopting behavior B. For instance, $\gamma(3)$ specifies the benefits (in adopting behavior B) that accrue to an arbitrary vertex $v \in \mathbf{V}'$ that has three neighbors. Let π_i denote the fraction of neighbors of v_i that have adopted behavior B. Let constants b_i and ρ_i be the agent-specific benefit and cost, respectively, for vertex v_i to adopt behavior B. Jackson and Yariv [10] state that node v_i switches to behavior B iff $\frac{b_i}{\rho_i} \cdot \gamma(d_i) \cdot \pi_i \geq 1$.

Returning to our cell-phone example, one could potentially use this model to describe the spread of the new plan. In this case, behavior A would be adherence to the current plan the user subscribes to, while B would be the use of the new plan. The associated SNDOP query would find a set of nodes which, if given a free plan, would jointly maximize the expected number of adoptees of the plan. Cost and benefit could be computed from factors such as income, time invested in switching plans, etc. We show how the model of [10] can be expressed via GAPs.

Diffusion Model 5.4.1 (Jackson-Yariv model) *Given a Jackson-Yariv model consisting of $\mathbf{G}' = (\mathbf{V}', \mathbf{E}')$, we can set up a social network $\mathscr{S} = (\mathbf{V}, \mathbf{E}', \ell_{vert}, \ell_{edge}, w)$ as follows. We define $\mathbf{E}'' = \{(x,y), (y,x) \mid (x,y) \in \mathbf{E}'\}$. We have a single edge predicate symbol edge which is assigned by ℓ_{edge} to every edge in $\mathbf{E}''$, and w assigns 1 to all edges in $\mathbf{E}''$. Our associated GAP Π_{JY} now consists of $\Pi_{\mathscr{S}}$ plus one rule of the following form for each vertex v_i:*

$$B(v_i) : \left\lfloor \frac{b_i}{\rho_i} \cdot \gamma\left(\sum_j E_j\right) \cdot \frac{\sum_j X_j}{\sum_j E_j} \right\rfloor \leftarrow \bigwedge_{v_j \mid \langle v_j, v_i \rangle \in \mathbf{E}''} (edge(v_j, v_i) : E_j \wedge B(v_j) : X_j)$$

It is easy to see that this rule (when applied in conjunction with $\Pi_{\mathscr{S}}$ for a social network $\mathscr{S}$) precisely encodes the Jackson-Yariv semantics.

5.4.2 Cascading Diffusion

In a **cascading** model, a vertex obtains a property from one of its neighbors, typically based on the strength of its relationship with the neighbor. These models were introduced in the epidemiology literature and perhaps the most well-known of these models, the SIR model, is more fully reviewed in Chap. 2. These cascading diffusion models have been applied to other domains as well. For example, Cha et al. [9] (diffusion of photos in Flickr) and Sun et al. [8] (diffusion of bookmarks in Facebook) both look at diffusion process in social networks as "social cascades" of this type.

The SIR Model of Disease Spread The SIR (*susceptible, infectious, removed*) model of disease spread (see Chap. 2) is a classic disease model which labels each vertex in a graph $G = (V, E)$ (of humans) with *susceptible* if it has not had the disease but can receive it from one of its neighbors, *infectious* if it has caught the disease and t_{rec} units of time have not expired, and *removed* when the vertex can no longer catch or transmit the disease. The SIR model assumes that a vertex v that is infected can transmit the disease to any of its neighbors v' with a probability $p_{v,v'}$ for t_{rec} units of time. It is assumed that becoming infected takes precisely a time unit. We would like to find a set of at most k vertices that would maximize the expected number of vertices that become infected. These are obviously good candidates to treat with appropriate medications. The following is a non-probabilistic variant of the SIR model represented as a GAP. Note it is not equivalent to the SIR model of Chap. 2—though it captures the intuition.

Diffusion Model 5.4.2 (SIR Model) *Let $\mathscr{S} = (V, E, \ell_{vert}, \ell_{edge}, w)$ be an SN where each edge is labeled with the predicate symbol e and $w(\langle v, v'\rangle) = p_{v,v'}$ assigns a probability of transmission to each edge . We use the predicate inf to designate the initially infected vertices. In order to create a GAP Π_{SIR} capturing the SIR model of disease spread, we first define t_{rec} predicate symbols $rec_1, \ldots, rec_{t_{rec}}$ where $rec_i(v)$ intuitively means that node v was infected i days ago. Hence, $rec_{t_{rec}}(v)$ means that v is "removed." We embed $\mathscr{S}$ into GAP Π_{SIR} by adding the following diffusion rules. If $t_{rec} > 1$, we add a non-ground rule for each $i = \{2, \ldots, t_{rec}\}$ - starting with t_{rec}:*

$$rec_i(V) : R \leftarrow rec_{i-1}(V) : R$$

$$rec_1(V) : R \leftarrow inf(V) : R$$

$$inf(V) : (1-R) \cdot P_{V',V} \cdot P_{V'} \cdot (1-R') \leftarrow rec_{t_{rec}}(V) : R \wedge e(V', V) : P_{V',V} \wedge$$
$$inf(V') : P_{V'} \wedge rec_{t_{rec}}(V') : R'.$$

The first rule says that if a vertex is in its $(i-1)$'th day of recovery with confidence R in the j'th iteration of the $\mathbf{T}_{\Pi_{SIR}}$ operator, then the vertex is i days into recovery (with the same confidence) in the $j + 1$'th iteration of the operator. Likewise, the second rule intuitively encodes the fact that if a vertex became infected with confidence R in the j'th iteration of the $\mathbf{T}_{\Pi_{SIR}}$ operator, then the vertex is one day into recovery in the $j + 1$'th iteration of the operator with the same confidence. The last rule says that if a vertex V' was infected with confidence $P_{V'}$ and has not been removed with confidence $1 - R'$, and there is an edge from V' to V in the social network (weighted with $P_{V',V}$), given the confidence $1 - R$ that V has not already been removed, then the confidence that the vertex V gets infected is $(1-R) \cdot P_{V',V} \cdot P_{V'}(1-R')$. Here, $P_{V'}(1-R')$ is one way of measuring the confidence that V' is infected and has not recovered and $P_{V',V}$ is the confidence of infecting the neighbor. Notice that e is a static property of the graph which does not change over the time, so we do not need time indexes for it. As for inf, the reason why we can avoid using time indexes is that we can keep track of how much time has gone since a vertex got infected with the predicates rec_i using the second rule.

Diffusion in the Flickr Photo Sharing Network The Flickr social network allows users to share photographs. Users create a list of "favorite" photos that can be viewed by other users. Cha et al. [9] use a variant of SIS above to study how photographs spread to the favorite lists of different users. A key difference is that they do not consider a node "recovered"—i.e. once a photo was placed on a favorite list, it was relatively permanent (the study was conducted over about 100 days). They also found that photos lower on a favorite list (as the result of a user marking a large number of photos as "favorite") for a given user could still spread through the network. A simple GAP that captures the intuition of how Flickr photos spread according to [9] uses just one rule:

Diffusion Model 5.4.3 (Flickr Photo Diffusion)

$$photo_i(V) : const_i \cdot X_i \leftarrow connected\_to(V', V) : 1 \land photo_i(V') : X_i$$

In Diffusion Model 5.4.3, the annotation of the vertex atom $photo_i(V)$ is the confidence that vertex V has marked photo i as one of its favorites. The predicate *connected_to* is the sole edge label representing that there is a connection from vertex V' to V (users select other users on this network). Additionally, the value $const_i$ is a number in $[0, 1]$ that determines how a given photo spreads in the network. Notice that the above rule is linear, as the head is a linear combination and $const_i \in [0, 1]$. We note that for all of these models, the annotation functions reflect one interpretation of the confidence that a vertex is infected or recovered—others are possible in our framework.

5.4.3 Homophilic Diffusion

Recently, [11] studied the spread of mobile application use on a global instant-messaging network of over 27 million vertices. They found that network-based diffusion could overestimate the spread of a mobile application and, for this scenario, over 50 % of the adopted use of the applications was due to **homophily**—vertices with similar properties adopting similar applications.

These results should not be surprising—the basic idea behind web-search advertising is that two users with a similar property (search term) will be interested in the same advertised item. In fact, Cha et al. [9] explicitly pre-processed their Flickr data set with a heuristic to *eliminate* properties attached to vertices that could not be accounted for by a diffusion process. We can easily represent homophilic diffusion in a GAP with the following type of diffusion rule:

Diffusion Model 5.4.4 (Homophilic Diffusion of a Product)

$$buys\_product(V) : 0.5 \times X \leftarrow property(V) : 1 \land exposed\_to\_product(V) : X$$

In Diffusion Model 5.4.4, if a vertex is exposed to a product (e.g. through mass advertising) and has a certain property, then the person associated with the vertex purchases the product with a confidence of $0.5 \times X$, where X measures the extent of the exposure. For this rule, there are no network effects.

In [10], the authors propose a "big seed" marketing approach that combines both homophilic and network effects. They outline a strategy of advertising to a large group of individuals who are likely to spread the advertisement further through network effects. We now describe a GAP that captures the ideas underlying big seed marketing. Suppose we have a set of vertex predicate symbols $\mathsf{AL} \subseteq \mathsf{VP}$ corresponding to people "attributes"—these may be certain demographic characteristics such as education level, race, level of physical fitness, etc. Suppose we want to advertise to people having (at least) one of $k \le |\mathsf{AL}|$ attributes to maximize an aggregate agg with respect to a goal predicate g (in other words, we want to choose k attributes and advertise to people having those attributes so that agg with respect to g is maximized). Consider the following construction.

Diffusion Model 5.4.5 (Big Seed Marketing) *The GAP includes an embedding of the social network as well as the network diffusion model of the user's choice. We make the following additions to the GAP and the SN:*

1. *Add vertex predicate symbol attrib to* VP.
2. *For each* $lbl \in \mathsf{AL}$, *add a vertex* v_{lbl} *to* $\mathbf{V}$. *We also set* $\ell_{vert}(v_{lbl}) = \{attrib\}$.
3. *For each* $lbl \in \mathsf{AL}$, *add the following non-ground rule:*

$$g(V) : \mathit{eff}_{lbl} \times X \leftarrow lbl(V) : 1 \wedge g(v_{lbl}) : X$$

where eff_{lbl} *is a constant in* $[0,1]$ *corresponding to the confidence that, if advertised to, a vertex* v *with attribute* lbl *obtains an annotation of* 1 *on* $g(v)$.

Our SNDOP query is $(agg, VC, k, g(V), g(V))$, *where* $VC = \{attrib(V) : 1\}$.

Note that in the above diffusion model, the v_{lbl} vertices correspond to advertisements directed toward different vertex properties. The VC condition forces the query to only return v_{lbl} vertices. As an example, a solution like $\{g(v_{lbl_1}), g(v_{lbl_2})\}$ means that we are targeting people having attribute lbl_1 or lbl_2. The diffusion rule, added per label, ensures that the mass advertisement is received and that the vertex acts accordingly (hence the eff_{lbl} constants).

5.5 Algorithmic Approach and Experiments

Regretfully, Theorem 5.2 precludes an exact solution in PTIME and Theorem 5.4 precludes a PTIME α-approximation algorithm where $\alpha < \frac{e}{e-1}$. Both of these results hold for the restricted case of linear-GAPs and positive-linear aggregate functions.

The good news is that we were able to show that (1) for linear-GAPs and a-priori VC queries with positive-linear aggregates, the *value* function is *submodular* (Theorem 5.1). (2) Under these conditions, we can reduce the problem to the maximization of a submodular function over a uniform matroid (the uniformity of the matroid is proved in Lemma 5.2 for a-priori VC queries). (3) We can leverage the work of [13] that admits a greedy $\frac{e}{e-1}$ approximation algorithm. In this section, we develop a greedy algorithm for SNDOP queries that leverages the above three results. This is analogous to the greedy approximation technique for the IC and LT models described in Chap. 4.

The **GREEDY-SNDOP** algorithm shown below assumes a linear GAP, an a-priori VC query with positive-linear aggregates, and a Normalized *value* function (notice that the latter requirement can be met as stated by Proposition 5.2). The algorithm provides $\frac{e}{e-1}$ approximation to the SNDOP query problem. As this matches the upper bound of Theorem 5.4, we cannot do better in terms of an approximation guarantee.

GREEDY-SNDOP$(\Pi, agg, VC, k, g_I(V), g_O(V))$ returns $SOL \subseteq \mathbf{V}$

1. Initialize $SOL = \emptyset$ and $REM = \{v \in \mathbf{V} \mid \left(\{g_I(v) : 1\} \cup \bigcup_{pred \in \ell_{vert}(v)} \{pred(v) : 1\} \right) \models VC[V/v]\}$
2. While $|SOL| < k$ and $REM \neq \emptyset$

   a. $v_{best} = $ null, $val = value(SOL)$, $inc = 0$
   b. For each $v \in REM$, do the following

      i. Let $inc_{new} = value(SOL \cup \{v\}) - val$
      ii. If $inc_{new} \geq inc$ then $inc = inc_{new}$ and $v_{best} = v$

   c. $SOL = SOL \cup \{v_{best}\}$, $REM = REM - \{v_{best}\}$

3. Return SOL

We now analyze the time complexity of **GREEDY-SNDOP**.

Proposition 5.3. *Given a SNDOP query* $Q = (agg, VC, k, g_I(V), g_O(V))$, *a social network* $\mathscr{S}$, *and a GAP* $\Pi \supseteq \Pi_{\mathscr{S}}$, *the complexity of* **GREEDY-SNDOP** *is* $O(k \cdot |\mathbf{V}| \cdot F(|\mathbf{V}|))$ *where* $F(|\mathbf{V}|)$ *is the time complexity to compute* $value(\mathbf{V})$ *for some set* $\mathbf{V} \subseteq \mathbf{V}$ *of size k.*

We note that most likely, the most expensive operation is the computation of *value* at line 2(b)i. One obvious way to address this issue is by using a non-ground version of the fixed-point.

Theorem 5.5. *Given a SNDOP query* $Q = (agg, VC, k, g_I(V), g_O(V))$, *a social network* $\mathscr{S}$, *and a GAP* $\Pi \supseteq \Pi_{\mathscr{S}}$, *if*

- Π *is a linear GAP,*
- Q *is a-priori VC,*
- *agg is positive-linear, and*
- *value is Normalized,*

then **GREEDY-SNDOP** *is an* $(\frac{e}{e-1})$*-approximation algorithm.*

We have implemented the GREEDY-SNDOP algorithm in 660 lines of Java code by re-using and extending the diffusion modeling Java library of [2] (approx 35 K lines of code). Our implementation uses multiple threads in the inner loop of the GREEDY-SNDOP algorithm to increase efficiency. All experiments were executed on the same machine with a dedicated 4-core 2.4 GHz processor and 22 GB of main memory. Times were measured to millisecond precision and are reported in seconds.

Data Set In order to evaluate GREEDY-SNDOP, we used a real-world dataset based on a social network of Wikipedia administrators and authors. Wikipedia is an online encyclopedia collaboratively edited by many contributors from all over the world. Selected contributors are given privileged administrative access rights to help maintain and control the collection of articles with additional technical features. A vote by existing administrators and ordinary authors determines whether an individual is granted administrative privileges. These votes are publicly recorded. Leskovec et al. [3] crawled 2794 elections from the inception of Wikipedia until January 2008. The votes casted in these elections give rise to a social network among Wikipedia administrators and authors by representing a vote of user i for user j as a directed edge from node i to j. In total, the dataset contains 103,663 votes (edges) connecting more than 7000 Wikipedia users (vertices). Hence, the network is large and densely connected.[9]

SNDOP-Query In our experiments, we consider the hypothetical problem of finding a set of administrators having the highest overall influence in the Wikipedia social network described above. We treat votes as a proxy for the inverse of influence. In other words, if user i voted for user j, we assume user j (intentionally through lobbying or unintentionally through the force of his contributions to Wikipedia) influenced user i to vote for him. All edges are assigned a weight of 1. Our SNDOP queries are designed as per the following definition.

Definition 5.15 (Wikipedia SNDOP-Query). Given some natural number $k > 1$, a Wikipedia SNDOP query, $WQ(k)$ is specified as follows:

- $agg = \mathsf{SUM}$—the intuition is that the aggregate provides us an expected number of vertices that are influenced.
- $VC = \emptyset$—we do not use a vertex condition in our experiments
- k as specified by the input
- $g_I(V) = g_O(V) = influenced(V)$

Diffusion Models Used We represented the diffusion process with two different models: one tipping and one cascading.

- **Cascading Diffusion Model** We used the Flickr Diffusion Model (Diffusion Model 5.4.3 on page 66) described in Sect. 5.4.2. In this model, a constant parameter α represents the "strength" or "likelihood" of influence. The larger the parameter α the higher the influence of a user on those who voted for her.

---

[9]Our Wikipedia data set does not include edge weights. However, including edge weights should not appreciably change the experimental results which show that solving SNDOP queries when tipping models are used is faster, in general, than when cascade models are used.

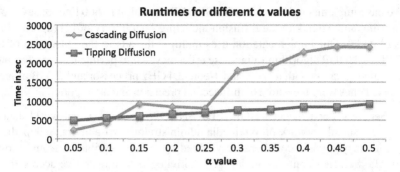

Fig. 5.2 Runtimes of GREEDY-SNDOP for different values of α and $k = 5$ in both diffusion models

- **Tipping Diffusion Model** Cha et al. [5] shows that there is a relationship between the likelihood of a vertex marking a photo as a favorite and the percentage of their neighbors that also marked that photo as a favorite. This implies a tipping-model (as in Sect. 5.4.1). We apply the Jackson-Yariv model with B equated to *influenced*. For each vertex $v_j \in \mathbf{V}$, we set the benefit to cost ratio $\left(\frac{b_j}{c_j}\right)$ to 1. Finally, the function γ defined in the Jackson Yariv model is the constant-valued function (for all values of x):

$$\gamma(x) = \alpha.$$

This says that irrespective of the number of neighbors that a vertex has, the benefit to adopting strategy B (i.e. *influenced*) is α. Therefore, the resulting diffusion rule for the linear Jackson-Yariv model is:

$$influenced(v) : \alpha \cdot \frac{\sum_j X_j}{|\{v_j | \langle v_j, v \rangle\}|} \leftarrow \bigwedge_{v_j | \langle v_j, v \rangle \in \mathbf{E}} influenced(v_j) : X_j$$

For both models, we derive a unique logic program for each setting of the parameter α. The parameter α depends on the application and can be learned from ground truth data. In our experiments, we varied α to avoid introducing bias.

Run-Time of GREEDY-SNDOP with Varying α and Different Diffusion Models Figure 5.2 shows the total runtime of GREEDY-SNDOP in seconds to find the set of $k = 5$ most influential users in the Wikipedia voting network for different values of the strength of influence parameter α. We varied α from 0.05 (very low level of influence) to 0.5 (very high level of influence) for both the cascading and tipping diffusion model. We observe that higher values of α lead to higher runtimes as expected since the scope of influence of any individual in the network is larger. Furthermore, we observe that the runtimes for the tipping diffusion model increase more slowly with α compared to the cascading model.

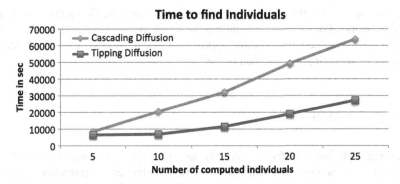

Fig. 5.3 Runtimes of GREEDY-SNDOP for different values of k and $\alpha = 0.2$ in both diffusion models

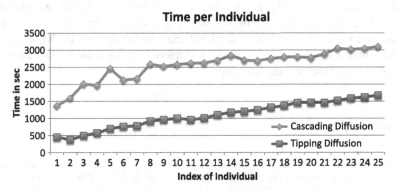

Fig. 5.4 Time per iteration of GREEDY-SNDOP for $\alpha = 0.2$ in both diffusion models

Run-Time of GREEDY-SNDOP with Varying k For the next set of experiments, we keep the strength of influence fixed to $\alpha = 0.2$ and varied k which governs the size of the set of influencers. Figure 5.3 reports the runtime of GREEDY-SNDOP for the query $WQ(k)$ with $k = 5, 10, 15, 20, 25$. For the cascading model, the runtime is approximately linear in k—a curve-fitting analysis using Excel showed a slight superlinear trend (even though the figure itself looks linear at first sight). Figure 5.4 shows the time taken to execute each of the 25 iterations of the outer loop for the query $WQ(25)$ with $\alpha = 0.2$. Note that each subsequent iteration is more expensive than the previous one since the size of the logic programs to consider increases with the addition of each ground atom $influenced(v_i)$. However, we also implemented the practical improvement of "lazy evaluation" of the submodular function as described in [7]. This improvement, which maintains correctness of the algorithms, stores previous improvements in total score and prunes the greedy search for the highest scoring vertex as discussed. We found that this technique also reduced the runtime of subsequent iterations.

Our experimental results show that we can answer SNDOP queries on large social networks. For example, computing the set of five most influential Wikipedia users in the voting network required approximately 2 h averaged over the different values of α in the tipping diffusion model.

5.6 Conclusion

Social networks are proliferating rapidly and have led to a wave of research on diffusion of phenomena in social networks. In this chapter, we introduce the class of *Social Network Diffusion Optimization Problems* (SNDOPs for short) which try to find a set of vertices (where each vertex satisfies some user specified vertex condition) that has cardinality k or less (for a user-specified $k > 0$) and that optimizes an objective function specified by the user in accordance with a diffusion model represented via the well-known generalized annotated program (GAP) framework. We have used specific examples of SNDOP queries drawn from product adoption (cell phone example) and epidemiology.

References

1. Subrahmanian, Venkatramana S., and Diego Reforgiato. "AVA: Adjective-verb-adverb combinations for sentiment analysis." Intelligent Systems, IEEE 23.4 (2008): 43–50.
2. Broecheler, Matthias, Paulo Shakarian, and V. S. Subrahmanian. "A scalable framework for modeling competitive diffusion in social networks." Social Computing (SocialCom), 2010 IEEE Second International Conference on. IEEE, 2010.
3. Leskovec, Jure, Daniel Huttenlocher, and Jon Kleinberg. "Predicting positive and negative links in online social networks." Proceedings of the 19th international conference on World wide web. ACM, 2010.
4. Shakarian, Paulo, et al. "Using generalized annotated programs to solve social network diffusion optimization problems." ACM Transactions on Computational Logic (TOCL) 14.2 (2013): 10.
5. Cha, Meeyoung, Alan Mislove, and Krishna P. Gummadi. "A measurement-driven analysis of information propagation in the flickr social network." Proceedings of the 18th international conference on World wide web. ACM, 2009.
6. Kifer, M., Subrahmanian, V.S., "Theory of generalized annotated logic programming and its applications." The Journal of Logic Programming, 12(4), 1992.
7. Leskovec, Jure, et al. "Cost-effective outbreak detection in networks." Proceedings of the 13th ACM SIGKDD international conference on Knowledge discovery and data mining. ACM, 2007.
8. Sun, Eric, et al. "Gesundheit! Modeling Contagion through Facebook News Feed." ICWSM. 2009.
9. Cha, Meeyoung, et al. "Characterizing social cascades in flickr." Proceedings of the first workshop on Online social networks. ACM, 2008.
10. Watts, Duncan J., Jonah Peretti, and Michael Frumin. Viral marketing for the real world. Harvard Business School Pub., 2007.

11. Distinguishing influence-based contagion from homophily-driven diffusion in dynamic networks
12. Goundan, Pranava R., and Andreas S. Schulz. "Revisiting the greedy approach to submodular set function maximization." Optimization online (2007): 1–25.
13. Nemhauser, George L., Laurence A. Wolsey, and Marshall L. Fisher. "An analysis of approximations for maximizing submodular set functions." Mathematical Programming 14.1 (1978): 265–294.
14. Feige, Uriel. "A threshold of ln n for approximating set cover." Journal of the ACM (JACM) 45.4 (1998): 634–652.
15. Hethcote, Herbert W. "Qualitative analyses of communicable disease models." Mathematical Biosciences 28.3 (1976): 335–356.
16. Cowan, Robin, and Nicolas Jonard. "Network structure and the diffusion of knowledge." Journal of economic Dynamics and Control 28.8 (2004): 1557–1575.
17. Watts, Duncan J. "Networks, dynamics, and the small-world phenomenon 1." American Journal of sociology 105.2 (1999): 493–527.
18. Rychtár, Jan, and Brian Stadler. "Evolutionary dynamics on small-world networks." International Journal of Computational and Mathematical Sciences 2.1 (2008): 1–4.
19. Lloyd, J. Foundations of Logic Programming. Berlin: Springer-Verlag, 1987.
20. Granovetter, Mark. "Threshold models of collective behavior." American journal of sociology (1978): 1420–1443.
21. Schelling, Thomas C. Micromotives and macrobehavior. WW Norton & Company, 2006.
22. Anderson, Roy M., and Robert M. May. "Population biology of infectious diseases: Part I." Nature 280 (1979): 361–7.
23. P. Shakarian, V.S. Subrahmanian, M.L. Sapino. Using Generalized Annotated Programs to Solve Social Network Optimization Problems. 26th Intl. Conference on Logic Programming (ICLP-10) (Jul. 2010).
24. Christoff, Z., Hansen, J.U., A logic for diffusion in social networks. Journal of Applied Logic, 13(1), 2015.
25. P. Shakarian, G.I. Simari, D. Callahan. Reasoning about Complex Networks: A Logic Programming Approach. 29th Intl. Conference on Logic Programming (ICLP-13) (Aug. 2013).
26. Kang, C., Molinaro, C., Kraus, S., Shavitt, Y., Subrahmanian, V.S. Diffusion Centrality in Social Networks. IEEE ASONAM, 2012.
27. Coelho, Flávio C., Oswaldo G. Cruz, and Cláudia T. Codeço. "Source Code for Biology and Medicine." Source code for biology and medicine 3 (2008): 3.

Chapter 6
Evolutionary Graph Theory

6.1 Introduction

Evolutionary graph theory (EGT), introduced by Lieberman et al. [17], studies the ability of a mutant gene to overtake a finite structured population. The reproduction of the individuals in the population is modeled as a stochastic process. The structure of the population is represented as a directed, weighted graph called an *evolutionary graph* (EG). Since its introduction, numerous results on EGT, both analytical and experimental, have been produced. Additionally, several extensions to the model have been proposed, including game-theoretic ones. The application of EGT to game theory has provided researchers new insight about the evolution of cooperation and other game-theoretic concepts in structured populations. In this chapter, we present the original model of [17] and various extensions. We also summarize major results in EGT (both analytical and experimental), including those relating to game theory. For a more comprehensive review of evolutionary graph theory, we suggest the previously-published review of [4], from which this chapter is based.

This chapter is organized as follows. In Sect. 6.2, we introduce the original model, discuss computation of fixation probability, and describe the standard game theoretic extensions. This is followed by a presentation of results concerning the computation of the fixation probability in Sect. 6.3 for graphs of certain topologies—including the large class of undirected EG's. Then we describe how some of the results relating to fixation probability change under alternative model dynamics in Sect. 6.4. We then survey more advanced game theoretic extensions in Sect. 6.5.

© The Author(s) 2015
P. Shakarian et al., *Diffusion in Social Networks*, SpringerBriefs
in Computer Science, DOI 10.1007/978-3-319-23105-1_6

6.2   Evolutionary Graph Theory Models

Consider a population of N individuals where there is no specified graph-structure relating them to each other (this is known as a *well-mixed* population). The *Moran Process* of [23] is a stochastic process used to model evolution in such a population. It is defined as follows. At each time-step a randomly selected individual is chosen to reproduce. Then, a second individual is chosen at random to die—replaced by a duplicate of the first individual. If all of the members of the population are identical (termed *residents* with fitness 1), and a mutant is introduced at random in the population (with fitness r, where $r = 1$ is the special case of *neutral drift*), the probability that the mutant will eventually overtake the population is known as the *fixation probability* (the opposite event—that all mutants die out—is called *extinction* and a population with a lower fixation probability is deemed more *evolutionarily stable* as it is resistant to invasion by a mutant). This probability, ρ_1, arising from this N original Moran Process, is often termed the *Moran probability* and can be solved for exactly (see Eq. (6.1)).

$$\rho_1 = \frac{1 - 1/r}{1 - 1/r^N} \tag{6.1}$$

In the original work that introduced EGT [17], Lieberman et al. generalize the model of the Moran Process by specifying relationships between the N individuals of the population in the form of a directed, weighted graph. We shall use the symbol V to denote the set of individuals. We can think of these individuals as vertices in a graph. The edges of the graph are specified by the adjacency matrix $W = [w_{ij}]$, where for vertices v_i, v_j, the quantity w_{ij} specifies the weight of the directed edge from v_i to v_j. As this is an evolutionary graph (EG), w_{ij} corresponds to the probability that, if v_i is selected to reproduce then it replaces v_j (note that for all v_i, $w_{ii} = 0$). Hence, for any given v_i, $\sum_j w_{ij} = 1$. The earlier work of [32] proves that, in such a structure if $\forall v_i, v_j \in V$ we have $w_{ij} = w_{ji}$, then the fixation probability for a randomly placed mutant is ρ_1. A similar result was proved in [18]. In [17], this result is extended for a wider variety of EG's where $\forall v_i$, $\sum_j w_{ij} = \sum_j w_{ji}$. This type of EG is known as *isothermal*. Consider the following theorem.

Theorem 6.1 (Isothermal Theorem [17]). *An EG is isothermal iff the fixation probability of a randomly placed mutant is ρ_1.*

Hence, for EG's that are not isothermal, the fixation probability of the evolutionary process is not only dependent on the fitness of the mutant (as in the Moran Process), but also on the structure of the graph.

6.2.1 Properties of Fixation Probability

Many researchers (such as [8, 20]) have studied the problem of computing the probability of fixation given that a certain subset of vertices are mutants. If the mutants inhabit set $C \subseteq V$, then this probability is written P_C. As the calculation of the fixation probability (ρ) for an EG is determined based on a uniformly picked vertex, we have the following relationship between ρ and P:

$$N \cdot \rho = \sum_i P_{\{v_i\}} \tag{6.2}$$

Note that although these two problems are closely related, they have rather different intuitions. The fixation probability ρ provides insight into a graph of a certain topology. For example, researchers often refer to graphs with a low value for ρ as being "evolutionary stable" as the topology of the graph seems to be resistant to a mutant invasion. The fixation probability P_C on the other hand tells us something about a set of vertices C. For example, identifying a certain subset C of a graph that has a higher fixation probability may cause a user to take a certain action regarding those vertices (dependent on the domain).

If the graph is not isothermal, but if we are under neutral drift, fixation probability P_C is additive. This was proven for the special case of undirected graphs in [7] and proved for general, weighted, directed graphs[5, 31].

Theorem 6.2 (Additive Under Neutral Drift [5, 31]). *When $r = 1$ for disjoint sets $C, D \subseteq V$, $P_C + P_D = P_{C \cup D}$.*

This additive result says that, under neutral drift, determining a subset of individuals in the population that maximize fixation probability is not (polynomially) harder than determining the fixation probability. Further, when we fix the topology of the graph, we find that for some subset of vertices C, that the fixation probability under neutral drift is a lower bound for the fixation probability when $r > 1$.

Theorem 6.3 (Neutral Drift as a Lower Bound [5, 31]). *For a given set C, let $P_C^{(1)}$ be the fixation probability under neutral drift and $P_C^{(r)}$ be the fixation probability calculated using a mutant fitness $r > 1$. Then, $P_C^{(1)} \leq P_C^{(r)}$.*

By Theorem 6.2 and Eq. (6.2), we observe that under neutral drift $\rho = 1/N$ regardless of the topology of the graph—even with directed and weighted edges. Hence, Theorem 6.3 tells us that for $r > 1$ we have $\rho \geq 1/N$. This particular observation is independently noted in [15]. In [19] the authors observe in their experiments that fixation probability monotonically increases with r.

As we can appeal to the Moran probability only in the case of an isothermal graph, we must resort to other calculations to determine ρ or P. Using the following set of constraints, we can solve directly for any P_C (hence, ρ as well by Eq. (6.2)).

$$P_C = \frac{\sum_{v_i \in C} \sum_{v_j \notin C} (r \cdot w_{ij} \cdot P_{C \cup \{v_j\}} + w_{ji} \cdot P_{C - \{v_i\}})}{\sum_{v_i \in C} \sum_{v_j \notin C} (r \cdot w_{ij} + w_{ji})}. \qquad (6.3)$$

These constraints originally appeared in [29] for the case of an undirected EG, but applies to the general case as it follows directly from the rules of dynamics. However, the number of constraints and variables is equal to the number of mutant-resident formations in the graphs, which is intractable for large N. In fact, [17] presents a decision problem related to computing the fixation probability that is claimed to be as hard as any problem in the complexity class NP (the class of nondeterministic polynomial time computable problems). In [7, 8] the authors attempt to reduce the number of constraints by finding automorphisms in the graph. Based on automorphism, the authors are able to calculate the exact number of possible mutant-resident formations (MRF's). Since this number gives the size of the system of linear equations for the fixation probability and in general increases with the difficulty of solving this system, the measure may be a useful indicator in deciding whether to undertake an analytical approach to solving for the fixation probability on a given graph. The authors then show that even in the special case of undirected EG's, if the graph contains a vertex of degree of at least 3, that there is a non-zero probability that the dynamics will evolve to any of the MRF's (except in the trivial cases where $C = V$ or $C = \emptyset$).[1] We note that for the general case, this still leads to an intractable number of constraints. Further, finding graph automorphisms is also a non-trivial problem in the general case (see [35] for the latest complexity results on graph automorphism).

Despite the computational difficulty of determining the fixation probability in the general case, there are several special classes of EG's where we have analytical solutions (or at least good approximations). We review many of these special cases in the next section. To address the issue of computation of the fixation probability in the general case (i.e., to confirm analytical approximations), most work we review resorts to simulation methods via Markov Chain Monte Carlo (MCMC). These simulations generally rely on a direct application of the model we have already described (see [29] for a pseudocode algorithm). However, as the size of the graph increases, even such simulations may become impractical. In [3], the authors address the issue of increasing the speed of such simulations. Their main technique for the general case is to stop the simulation early if the number of mutants in the population exceed a certain threshold (hence that particular simulation would be considered to have reached fixation). They determine this threshold by finding the conditional probability that mutants spread to M vertices in the graph given that extinction eventually occurs. The authors plot the probability distribution density of this function compared to M and determine for several types of networks (including E-R graphs) of size 10^3, that if $M > 10^2$ then this probability drops to 10^{-5}—which is lower than the estimated standard error of a MCMC simulation by several orders

---

[1]There is the exception of an alternating state where every edge connects a mutant-resident pair. This state cannot be reached if it exists.

of magnitude (the authors show that the estimated standard error for populations of 10^4 to 10^6 have associated standard errors of at least 10^{-4}). Hence, the outcome of any simulation where the number of mutants exceeds 100 is considered equivalent to fixation. The authors showed that for networks with 10^3 and 10^4 vertices, and showed it provided a significant speed-up of up to 100 times, depending on the size of the network.

In change to [5, 31], the authors introduce a novel approach that can quickly compute the fixation probability in an evolutionary graph (with weights and directions) under neutral drift. We rely on the idea of a *vertex probability*—the probability of a given vertex being a mutant. In the limit of time, these probabilities converge to the fixation probability (for strongly connected graphs). We have shown that this convergence occurs quickly in practice, providing an improvement over MCMC by several orders of magnitude. While this result is for the case of neutral drift, Theorem 6.3 suggests it may provide good insight for $r > 1$. Further, the quick convergence of our algorithm in practice may also suggest that having a value of $r \neq 1$ may be a source of complexity.

Another recent development is the work of Houchmandzadeh and Vallade who use dynamics to quickly approximate fixation probability in a certain bi-level graph that generalizes the model of [18]. While this particular model can also generalize the standard evolutionary graphs of [17]. However, it is unclear if their approximation is still appropriate for arbitrary graphs.

6.2.2 Game Theoretic Extensions

One of the most popular applications of EGT is game theory. In the game theoretic context, vertices of a graph represent agents and edges represent potential for interaction between them. Interactions between agents are games played that can be described using a normal game theoretic payoff matrix. EGT thus provides a structural component for interactions in populations of agents. Evolutionary game theory, which is concerned with the population-dependent success of game theoretic strategies, has initially mostly focused on well-mixed populations in which interactions between all agents are equally likely. Incorporating EGT to evolutionary game theory can take into account the effect of population structure, which has the capacity to crucially impact evolutionary trajectories, outcomes, and strategy success. Thus EGT is a welcome tool to explore how many of the results for well-mixed populations are affected by population structure.

In game-theoretic applications of EGT, the evolutionary fitness (f_i) of individual v_i is often related to their game theoretic payoff (P) (based on game-play with neighbors) with something akin to the following equation:

$$f_i = 1 - w + w \cdot P \tag{6.4}$$

The parameter w relates the payoff acquired from games played to fitness. If $w = 1$, the payoff acquired is equal to the fitness. If $w = 0$, the game is irrelevant and we are at neutral drift. An often explored special case is *weak selection*, where $w \ll 1$, which reflects the assumption that the game of interest plays only a partial role in the overall fitness of individuals. Using this paradigm, researchers have reached a variety of important conclusions on the effects of population structure on game-theoretic concepts.

Evolutionary game dynamics of finite populations on graphs for a general two-player game between mutants and residents are often considered using the following payoff matrix:

$$\begin{array}{c|cc} & \text{mutant} & \text{resident} \\ \hline \text{mutant} & a & b \\ \text{resident} & c & d \end{array} \qquad (6.5)$$

Tarnita et al. [34] consider evolutionary dynamics (under weak selection) on graphs for the general game given by (6.5) and present a theorem stating that a strategy A (mutant) is favored over strategy B (resident) iff $\sigma a + b > c + \sigma d$, depending on the single parameter σ. "A is favored over B" means that it is more abundant in the stationary distribution of the mutation selection process. The authors show σ to depend on the population structure, update rule (see Sect. 6.4), and mutation rate. Thus the single parameter can be used to quantify the ability of a population structure to promote the evolution of cooperation or to choose efficient equilibria in coordination games. In general, if the combination of update rule and population structure leads to a $\sigma > 1$ (which can but does not necessarily occur for different combinations), individuals of the same strategy type are more likely to interact due to a clustering of strategies [24, 25].

In Sect. 6.5 we will review other important work considering various aspects of game theoretic applications of EGT.

6.3 Determining Fixation Probability for Fixed Fitness

We now turn to the problem of determining fixation probability for some special cases of graphs when the value of r is fixed (i.e., most non-game theoretic work). First we look at computing fixation probabilities for graphs of certain topologies. Then, we look at a very large special case—that of undirected graphs.

6.3.1 Fixation Probability Calculations for Certain Topologies

In [17], the authors examine the fixation probability for a few special cases of EG's to illustrate how fixation can be amplified or suppressed based on the structure of the

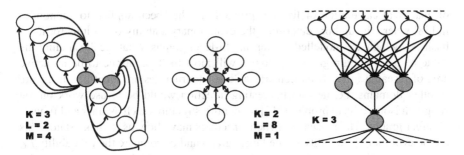

Fig. 6.1 *Left*: Super-star EG, $K = 3, L = 2, M = 4$. *Center*: Star EG, $K = 2, L = 8, M = 1$. *Right*: Funnel EG, $K = 3$

graph. For example, they define a *one-rooted* graph as a graph with a unique global source without incoming edges (i.e., a directed tree, with edges directed toward the leaves, would be such a graph—the unique global source being the root in this case). Hence, for any value of r, if an EG is one-rooted its fixation probability is $1/N$.

Another special case is the EG referred to as a *super-star* (see Fig. 6.1). Such a structure, denoted $S_{L,M}^K$ consists of a central vertex, v_{center} surrounded by L leaves. A leaf ℓ, contains M *reservoir* vertices, $r_{\ell,m}$ and $K - 2$ ordered chain vertices $c_{\ell,1}, \ldots, c_{\ell,K-2}$. All directed edges are of the form $(r_{\ell,m}, c_{\ell,1})$, $(c_{\ell,w}, c_{\ell,w+1})$, $(c_{\ell,K-2}, v_{center})$, and $(v_{center}, r_{\ell,m})$. Denoting the fixation probability of EG $S_{L,M}^K$ as $\rho(S_{L,M}^K)$, the following result is given in [17].

$$\lim_{L,M \to \infty} \rho(S_{L,M}^K) = \frac{1/r}{1 - 1/r^{K \cdot N}} \tag{6.6}$$

Because of the role it plays in enhancing fixation, the K parameter is often referred to as the *amplification factor*. If $K = 2$, this is simply referred to as a *star* EG (see Fig. 6.1). Another special case, related to the super-star, is the funnel (see Fig. 6.1). A generalization of the funnel, known as a *layered network* was studied in [2, 3]. In this type of EG, V can be partitioned into K subsets $V_1, \ldots, V_K$ such that for all $v \in V_i$ there are only outgoing edges to vertices in set $V_{i+1 mod K}$. Barbosa et al. also presents a way to increase the speed of MCMC simulations specific to layered networks in [3]. Their technique involves skipping evolutionary steps where none of the vertices in the graph changes a label. This is done by calculation the probability of a change occurring somewhere in the graph. The tradeoff with this speed-up is the price of calculating this probability compared to the savings. The authors show for layered networks, that this probability can be efficiently computed and yield a 2–3 times speed-up in simulations for K-funnels and random layered networks.

These special cases represent important building blocks for other results. For instance, [6] leverages some of these intuitions to study fixation probability for games on star graphs while the work on bi-level EG's. More recently, this style of analytical calculation of fixation probabilities has been applied to economics in [38] where the authors determine the evolutionary stability of various forms of business, which are modelled as star and bi-level graphs. Analytically finding the value of ρ for certain graph topologies will most likely continue to be an active area of research in EGT, particularly as certain structures are identified in nature or other domains. Perhaps an interesting direction would be to use work on the subgraph isomorphism problem [12] to identify structures such as stars and funnels in larger graphs. The presence of such structures may allow us to make statements on the evolutionary stability of the larger graph and/or compare the probability P_C for certain vertices in the larger graph (i.e., P_C may be higher for a set of nodes located in a star substructure of a larger graph).

6.3.2   Undirected Evolutionary Graphs

Several work explore: undirected EG's. In this case, we shall use the symbol E to denote the set of edges. However, it is important to note that the precise definition of this graph is somewhat different than the standard concept of an undirected graph. Specifically, the weights in both directions are not the same. This is defined by Broom and Rychtar [8] as

$$w_{ij} = \begin{cases} d_i^{-1} & \textit{iff } (v_i, v_j) \in E \textit{ or } (v_j, v_i) \in E \\ 0 & \textit{otherwise} \end{cases} \tag{6.7}$$

where d_i is the degree of v_i. The intuition behind this asymmetric assignment of weights is that if v_i is chosen to reproduce, it replaces one of its neighbors with a uniform probability. In [8], the authors determine a necessary and sufficient condition for an isothermal undirected graph.

Theorem 6.4 (Undirected Isothermal Theorem [8]). *An undirected EG is isothermal iff it is regular.*

Interestingly, for the undirected case, when $r = 1$ (neutral drift), there is a tractable solution to the constraints specified by Eq. (6.3) that is presented in [7].

$$P_C = \frac{\sum_{v_i \in C}(d_i^{-1})}{\sum_{v_j \in V}(d_j^{-1})} \tag{6.8}$$

Hence, for an undirected graph with $r = 1$, we have $\rho = 1/N$. For the case where a mutant is very advantageous, $r \gg 1$, [9] provides us with an approximation for P_C when C is a singleton set (the approximation is based on the assumption that once $|C| \geq 2$, then fixation occurs).

$$P_{\{v_i\}} \approx \frac{r}{r + \sum_{v_j \in V - \{v_i\}} w_{ji}} \tag{6.9}$$

The authors of [9] conducted an exhaustive study of undirected graphs with eight vertices and concluded that a low degree of a vertex corresponded with a more advantageous mutant and this advantage seemed to increase monotonically for vertex v_i with $\frac{\sum_{v_j \in V} d_j}{N} - d_i$. This aligns well with Eqs. (6.8) and (6.9). Further, they also provide the following analytical approximation for relative mutant advantage.

$$\frac{P_{\{v_i\}}}{P_{\{v_j\}}} \approx \left(\frac{d_j}{d_i}\right)^2 \tag{6.10}$$

The inverse relationship between fixation and the degree of the initial mutant vertex shown by Broom et al. [9] is in strong agreement with the previous work of [1]. It is interesting to note that experimentally, it was observed in [9] that as the relative fitness of the mutant increases, the fixation probabilities increase more rapidly for mutants placed into vertices with higher degree. Some of these results were experimentally verified in [10]. In Sect. 6.4, we examine the correlation of the initial mutant's degree to the fixation probability when the dynamics of the evolutionary process is changed via different update rules.

It is also interesting to note that the authors of [8] were able to analytically solve for the fixation probabilities for the special case of undirected star graphs ($K = 2$) of L leaf vertices (hence $N = L + 1$). Let P_i^0 (P_i^0) denote the fixation of probability given i mutants on the leaves and the center being a mutant (resp. the center being a resident). Broom and Rychtar [8] derive the following.

$$P_1^0 = \frac{1}{1 + \frac{L}{L+r} \sum_{j=1}^{L-1} \left(\frac{L+r}{r(L \cdot r + 1)}\right)^j} \tag{6.11}$$

$$P_0^0 = \frac{r}{r+L} P_1^0 \quad P_0^0 = \frac{r \cdot L}{r \cdot L + 1} P_1^0 \tag{6.12}$$

From this, they derive the following for fixation probability ($\rho_{undir\text{-}star}$).

$$\rho_{undir\text{-}star} = \frac{L \cdot \frac{r \cdot L}{r \cdot L + 1} + \frac{r}{r+L}}{(L+1)\left(1 + \frac{L}{L+r} \sum_{j=1}^{L-1} \left(\frac{L+r}{r(L \cdot r + 1)}\right)^j\right)} \tag{6.13}$$

$$\lim_{L \to \infty} \rho_{undir\text{-}star} = \frac{1 - \frac{1}{r^2}}{1 - \frac{1}{r^{2L}}} \tag{6.14}$$

6.4 Alternate Update Rules

Let us momentarily return to the original model of [17]. At each time-step, some vertex v_i is selected with probability $\frac{f_i}{\sum_{v_j \in V} f_j}$, where f_i is the fitness of v_i and equal to either 1 or r. This is the vertex chosen to reproduce, hence a 'birth' event. The next vertex selected is one of the neighbors of v_i—lets call it v_j and it is selected with probability w_{ij}. This is a 'death' event as v_j is replaced with a duplicate of v_i. Notice that the fitness of v_j is not considered when it is selected. Hence, the fitness bias is on the birth event. This method of selecting vertices v_i and v_j is referred to as an *update rule*. The update rule described in [17] is termed 'birth-death with birth bias' or BD-B updating. Several works address different update rules including: [1, 19, 20, 27, 33]. Overall, we have identified three major families of update rules— birth-death (a.k.a. the invasion process) where the vertex to reproduce is chosen first, death-birth (a.k.a. the voter model) where the vertex to die is chosen first, and link dynamics, where an edge is chosen. We summarize these in Table 6.1.

Note that the three categories of Table 6.1 are very broad as they do not consider fitness-based bias in vertex selection (i.e., the BD-B updating of [17] places the bias on the birth event as the first vertex is chosen with a probability proportional to its fitness). If there is a birth-bias, the individual reproducing is chosen with a probability proportional to its fitness. If there is a death-bias, the individual dying is chosen with a probability inversely proportional to its fitness. We summarize how directionality and bias affect the update rules in Table 6.2. Note that imitation (IM) is also known as *biased link dynamics*.

For the case on undirected graphs, there are many results based on the initial placement of the mutant have been discovered for several update rules (as we have described for BD-B in the previous section). In [1, 33], the authors study moments of degree distribution, density, and degree-weighted moments and show that the fixation probability is proportional to the average degree-weighted moment for death-birth updating (a.k.a. voter model), the inverse for birth-death (a.k.a. invasion process), and equal to the density (the percentage of the number of vertices in the

Table 6.1 Different families of update rules

Update rule	Intuition
Birth-Death (BD)	(1) vertex v_i selected
(a.k.a. Invasion process (IP))	(2) Neighbour of v_i, vertex v_j selected
	(3) Offspring of v_i replaces v_j
Death-Birth (DB)	(1) vertex v_i selected
(a.k.a. Voter model (VM))	(2) Neighbour of v_i, vertex v_j selected
	(3) Offspring of v_j replaces v_i
Link dynamics (LD)	(1) Edge (v_i, v_j) selected
	(2) The offspring of one vertex in the edge replaces the other vertex

Table 6.2 Variations of EGT

Update rule	Special case	Intuition
Birth-Death (BD)	Unbiased, undirected	Offspring of v_i replace v_j
	Directed	Considers v_i's outgoing edges
	Biased-birth (BD-B)	v_i chosen w. prob. proportional to f_i
	Biased-death (BD-D)	v_j chosen w. prob. proportional to f_j^{-1}
Death-Birth (DB)	Unbiased, undirected	Offspring of v_j replace v_i
	Directed	Considers v_i's incoming edges
	Biased-birth (DB-B)	v_j chosen w. prob. proportional to f_j
	Biased-death (DB-D)	v_i chosen w. prob. proportional to f_i^{-1}
Link Dyn. (LD)	Unbiased, undirected	One vertex reproduces to replace the other
	Imitation (IM)	Least fit vertex dies, replaced by offspring of other vetex
	Pairwise Compar. (PC)	v_j replaces v_i iff $f_j > f_x$, o/w no change
	Directed, unbiased	Edge from v_i to v_j, v_i replaces v_j
	Directed, birth biased	Edge selected w. prob. proportional to f_i
	Directed, death biased	Edge selected w. prob. proportional to f_j^{-1}

v_i and v_j are vertices in a graph that are neighbors, v_i is always chosen first. f_i and f_j are the associated fitness values which both equal 1 in the case of neutral drift

Table 6.3 Relationship between fixation and degree of initial vertex (undirected graphs)

Update rule	Fixation probability proportional to
BD-B	Inverse of degree of initial vertex
DB-D	Degree of initial vertex
LD	Density of mutant vertices

graph labeled as mutants) for link dynamics, thus independent of the underlying graph in that case. Note that their results for BD-B are in agreement with the finding of [9] described earlier (Table 6.3).

As shown in Theorem 6.4, under BD-B, an undirected EG is isothermal iff it is regular. In [1], this is extended to other update rules as follows.

Theorem 6.5 ([1]). *Evolutionary dynamics under BD-B, DB-D, and LD are equivalent for undirected regular EG's.*

Although there is currently an excellent suit of results for studying evolutionary graphs under various different update rules in the directed case, there has been no work (to the knowledge of the authors) that compares any of these update rules to the synchronous update model described by Santos et al. in [30]. At each time-step, all individuals in the population update their labels (i.e., mutant or resident, or strategy if game-play is involved) simultaneously. For each vertex v_i, one of its neighbors (vertex v_j) is selected at $\frac{1}{d_i}$. Then, if and only if $f_j > f_i$, v_i's label is replaced with v_j's label with a probability proportional to $f_j - f_i$ (i.e., $\frac{f_j - f_i}{\max(d_i, d_j) \cdot r}$ for example). There are several interesting aspects about this model. For instance, the fitness of vertices does not play a role in selecting which vertex is born and/or dies. Rather, the fitness determines if a vertex is replaced by a neighbor and the probability at which this happens. Additionally, as all vertices are updated simultaneously, we might conjecture that the evolutionary process occurs faster than in the other update rules. These topics may warrant some further consideration in that synchronous updates may represent some real-world processes more accurately or possibly be used as a proxy for the standard update rules we have already described. Further, the synchronous update model can also easily be extended to the directed case, which we cover for the other update rules in the next section.

Not only does the original model of [17] utilize a directed graph, but many real-world networks can be more accurately modeled as directed graphs than undirected ones. This is the motivation of the work [19, 20]. There are two main conclusions to their work: (1) degree correlation to fixation probability (i.e., using the exact methods of [7] or the mean-field approximation) for undirected graphs does not necessarily hold in the direct case and (2) directed graphs generally suppress fixation more than undirected ones.

In [20], the authors study directed graphs under LD, BD, and DB for $r = 1$. For all three update rules, under $r = 1$, they derive sets of linear constraints using the mean-field approximation (degrees of connected vertices in the EG are uncorrelated). They compare these analytical approximations with experiments and find that, in general, the fixation probability is not only dependent on the degree of the initial vertex but also the global structure of the graph. In fact, often there is no observed relation between degree and fixation. See Table 6.4 for a summary of experimental results compared with the analytical approximations. While [20] mainly considers the case of neutral drift ($r = 1$), they also run some tests with $r = 4$ and claim that fixation increases monotonically with r.

In [19], the authors perform an in-depth comparison on directed and undirected networks for several variants of these rules. He exactly computes fixation probabilities on an exhaustive set of small graphs (with six vertices) and uses Monte-Carlo approximation for randomly generated larger graphs. He found that directed networks tended to suppress more than undirected, regardless of update rule. Based on these experiments for small networks, the order of amplification for rules is as follows: BD-B > LD > DB-D > BD-D > DB-B (BD-B was least suppressive and DB-B was the most suppressive). The value of r was set to 4 in these trials. For large graphs (also with $r = 4$), the simulations provided the following ordering: BD-B > BD-D, LD > DB-D > DB-B.

Table 6.4 Summary of experimental results for directed case with $r = 1$ in [20] illustrating whether experimentally-determined fixation probability results that aligned with the mean-field approximation

Mean-field approximation	BD: $1/d_{in}$	DB: d_{out}	LD: d_{out}/d_{in}
Asymmetric random	$1/d_{in}$	d_{out}	d_{out}/d_{in}
Asymmetric scale-free	No relation	d_{out}	d_{out}/d_{in}
E-mail	No relation	No relation	No relation
Asymmetric small world	No relation	No relation	No relation

d_{in} and d_{out} are the in and out degrees of the initial mutant vertex

6.5 Further Game Theoretic Results

Now that we have described alternate update rules, we shall re-visit our game-theoretic extensions and review some results regarding topics such as cooperation, reciprocity, and evolutionary stability w.r.t. a game on the graph under various update rules.

6.5.1 Evolutionary Stability on Graphs

Evolutionary stability, describing the ability of a player type comprising a population to be resistant against invasion by another type, is an important concept in evolutionary game theory that has been well studied for well-mixed populations. Ohtsuki et al. [28] analyze evolutionary stability on regular graphs of degree $k > 2$ for the BD, DB, and IM updating rules through pairwise approximation and simulation. Evolutionary stability on graphs means that a small fraction of rare mutants cannot spread, i.e., a resident strategy evolutionarily stable if it has a selective advantage over an invading strategy (invading at an ε fraction of the total population). Ohtsuki et al. provide evolutionary stability conditions for this definition on regular graphs for the different update rules considered, and (on top of the game payoff matrix values) all these conditions depend on the graph degree k. The results are validated through simulations on specific game examples. The important point to consider from these results is that population structure can have crucial impact on the evolutionary stability of strategies, i.e., in the words of "traditional criterion for evolutionarily stable strategies in well-mixed populations is neither necessary nor sufficient to guarantee evolutionary stability in structured populations".

6.5.2 Regular Graphs and the Replicator Equation

Ohtsuki et al. [27] study evolutionary games on regular graphs of degree k considering the BD, DB, IM, PC update rules.[2] The authors use pair approximation [14, 16, 21, 22, 36] to derive a system of ordinary differential equations describing the change in expected frequency of strategies in a game on a graph over time. In the limit of *weak selection* ($w \ll 1$), the authors show that under the update rules BD, DB, and IM this differential equation is the well-known replicator equation with a transformed payoff matrix. The payoff matrix is the original payoff matrix summed with a payoff matrix describing the local competition of strategies, different for BD,

---

[2]We use the shorter BD and DB notation for the update rules with birth bias BD-B and DB-B. See Table 6.2.

DB, and IM. PC is shown to be equivalent to BD in the model used. This result is applied to the Prisoner's Dillema and the Snow Drift Game on regular graphs. Results for the Prisoner's Dillema coincide with those of [26], showing identical conditions necessary for cooperators to be favored over defectors.

6.5.3   Evolution of Cooperation and Social Viscosity

Ohtsuki et al. [26] explore the problem of cooperation on a variety of graphs through numerical simulations. The graph types explored are cycles, spatial lattices, random regular graphs, random graphs and scale free networks. Every player plays a game with all its neighbors, where the game between two players is given by the payoff matrix (6.15) below. This game represents a Prisoner's Dilemma game between two players, and gives a kind of Public Goods Game when each player plays the game with all its neighbors. In this game b is called the benefit of the altruistic act and c is the cost of the altruistic cooperation act. A Cooperator that is connected to n Cooperators and m Defectors for receives a payoff of $bn - c(n+m)$.

$$
\begin{array}{c|cc}
 & \text{cooperate} & \text{defect} \\
\hline
\text{cooperate} & b - c & -c \\
\text{defect} & b & 0
\end{array}
\qquad (6.15)
$$

Ohtsuki et al.'s results suggests that under the DB update rule, a necessary condition for cooperation to arise in the types of graphs explores is that $b/c > k$, where k is the average number of neighbors. This result is derived under the conditions of weak selection and that the number of vertices in the graph is much larger than the average degree. The authors note the close and interesting relation of this result to Hamilton's rule [13], which states that kin selection can favor cooperation provided that $b/c > 1/r$, where r is the coefficient of genetic relatedness between individuals. The condition for cooperation fits less well for non-regular graphs, as one would expect due to the larger variance in vertex degrees, but is a good approximation unless the variance in degree distributions of the graph gets too large. Other dynamics explored are IM,[3] for which cooperation is favored when $b/c > k + 2$, and BD, for which cooperation is never favored by selection.

6.5.4   Graph Heterogeneity and Evolution of Cooperation

Santos et al. [30] investigate the effects of single-scale and scale-free networks on cooperation in the Prisoner's Dillema, Snow-Drift, and Stag-Hunt games through

---

[3]The authors of [26] also note that mathematically, "IM updating can be obtained from DB updating by adding loops to every vertex".

simulations. The update rule used is a type of imitation dynamic in which all vertices update simultaneously in each generation, as follows: for each vertex a random neighbor is chosen, and if that neighbor has achieved a higher payoff, the vertex adopts the strategy of this neighbor with a probability proportional to the payoff difference. The authors find that in degree-heterogeneous graphs cooperation is easier to sustain than in well-mixed populations and thus identify heterogeneity as a "powerful mechanism for the emergence of cooperation." Additionally, the authors find that the sustainability of cooperation also depends on "detailed and intricate ties" between agents. As evidence of this, scale free networks which exhibit properties like those that emerge from models of growth from preferential attachment (Albert-Barbarasi topology) are shown to produce higher cooperation than random scale-free networks.

Fu et al. [11] devise a framework for the general study of games on arbitrary graphs under weak selection, formulating the game dynamics as a discrete Markov process. Using DB updating and the game of the prisoner's dilemma, they employ their method on random regular graphs and scale-free networks to demonstrate the utility of their framework compared to pair-approximation and simulated data. The authors find a stronger correlation between their approach and the simulated results. They also reach some conclusions on the evolution of cooperation, most notably that under DB updating and weak selection, degree heterogeneous graphs (e.g., scale-free networks) generally impose higher invasion barriers than regular graphs. This extends a result in [1] reporting that a heterogeneous graph is an inhospitable environment for a mutant to evolve in the case of constant selection. Fu et al. show this to be true for weak selection as well. This result seems to be in disagreement with the conclusion of [30], which concludes that graph heterogeneity aids the emergence of cooperation. Fu et al. point out that this conclusion by Santos et al. [30] hinges on the simultaneous appearance of a number of cooperators to overcome the invasion barrier.

6.6 Conclusion

In this chapter, we have described *evolutionary graph theory*, which was first introduced in [17] and generalizes the classic Moran process of [23]. We have described the original model, the major results and extensions, and applications to game theory. A somewhat recent trend in the area of evolutionary graph theory is applied work such as [38] for economics and [37] in biology most likely represent just the beginning of a new trend. Further, the desire to add realism to diffusion models extends beyond EGT and is currently an active topic relating to nearly every model in this book. In the next chapter, we review some empirical results toward this end.

References

1. Antal, T., Redner, S., Sood, V., 2006. Evolutionary dynamics on degree-heterogeneous graphs. Physical Review Letters 96 (18), 188104. http://link.aps.org/abstract/PRL/v96/e188104
2. Barbosa, V. C., Donangelo, R., Souza, S. R., 2009. Network growth for enhanced natural selection. Physical Review E (Statistical, Nonlinear, and Soft Matter Physics) 80 (2), 026115. http://link.aps.org/abstract/PRE/v80/e026115
3. Barbosa, V. C., Donangelo, R., Souza, S. R., Oct 2010. Early appraisal of the fixation probability in directed networks. Phys. Rev. E 82 (4), 046114.
4. P. Shakarian, P. Roos, A. Johnson. A Review of Evolutionary Graph Theory with Applications to Game Theory. BioSystems 107(2), 2012.
5. P. Shakarian, P. Roos, G. Moores. A Novel Analytical Method for Evolutionary Graph Theory Problems. BioSystems. 111(2), 2015.
6. Broom, M., Hadjichrysanthou, C., Rychtar, J., 2010. Evolutionary games on graphs and the speed of the evolutionary process. Proceedings of the Royal Society A 466, 1327–1346.
7. Broom, M., Hadjichrysanthou, C., Rychtar, J., Stadler, B. T., Apr. 2010. Two results on evolutionary processes on general non-directed graphs. Proceedings of the Royal Society A: Mathematical, Physical and Engineering Sciences 466 (2121), 2795–2798. http://rspa.royalsocietypublishing.org
8. Broom, M., Rychtar, J., May 2008. An analysis of the fixation probability of a mutant on special classes of non-directed graphs. Proceedings of the Royal Society A 464, 2609–2627.
9. Broom, M., Rychtar, J., Stadler, B., 2011. Evolutionary dynamics on graphs - the effect of graph structure and initial placement on mutant spread. Journal of Statistical Theory and Practice 5 (3), 369–381.
10. Broom, M., Rychtar, J., Stadler, B., 2009. Evolutionary dynamics on small-order graphs. Journal of Interdisciplinary Mathematics 12 (2), 129–140.
11. Fu, F., Wang, L., Nowak, M. A., Hauert, C., Apr. 2009. Evolutionary dynamics on graphs: Efficient method for weak selection. Physical Review E 79 (4).
12. Garey, M. R., Johnson, D. S., 1979. Computers and Intractability; A Guide to the Theory of NP-Completeness. W. H. Freeman & Co., New York, NY, USA.
13. Hamilton, W., 1964. The genetical evolution of social behaviour. II* 1. Journal of theoretical biology 7 (1), 17–52.
14. Haraguchi, Y., Sasaki, A., 2000. The evolution of parasite virulence and transmission rate in a spatially structured population. Journal of Theoretical Biology 203 (2), 85–96.
15. Houchmandzadeh, B., Vallade, M., July 2011. The fixation probability of a beneficial mutation in a geographically structured population. New Journal of Physics 13 (7), 073020. http://stacks.iop.org/1367-2630/13/i=7/a=073020
16. Keeling, M., 1999. The effects of local spatial structure on epidemiological invasions. Proceedings: Biological Sciences 266 (1421), 859–867.
17. Lieberman, E., Hauert, C., Nowak, M. A., 2005. Evolutionary dynamics on graphs. Nature 433 (7023), 312–316. http://dx.doi.org/10.1038/nature03204
18. Maruyama, T., 1974. A simple proof that certain quantities are independent of the geographical structure of population. Theoretical Population Biology 5 (2), 148–154. http://www.sciencedirect.com/science/article/pii/0040580974900379
19. Masuda, N., 2009. Directionality of contact networks suppresses selection pressure in evolutionary dynamics. Journal of Theoretical Biology 258 (2), 323–334.
20. Masuda, N., Ohtsuki, H., 2009. Evolutionary dynamics and fixation probabilities in directed networks. New Journal of Physics 11, 033012.
21. Matsuda, H., Ogita, N., Sasaki, A., Sato, K., 1992. Statistical mechanics of population. Prog. Theor. Phys 88 (6), 1035–1049.
22. Matsuda, H., Tamachi, N., Sasaki, A., N., O., 1987. A lattice model for population biology. In: Mathematical Topics in Biology, Morphogenesis and Neuro-sciences. Vol. 71 of Springer Lecture Notes in Biomathematics. pp. 154–161.

23. Moran, P., 1958. Random processes in genetics. Mathematical Proceedings of the Cambridge Philosophical Society 54 (01), 60–71.
24. Nowak, M., May, R., 1992. Evolutionary games and spatial chaos. Nature 359 (6398), 826–829.
25. Nowak, M., Tarnita, C., Antal, T., 2010. Evolutionary dynamics in structured populations. Philosophical Transactions of the Royal Society B: Biological Sciences 365 (1537), 19.
26. Ohtsuki, H., Hauert, C., Lieberman, E., Nowak, M. A., May 2006. A simple rule for the evolution of cooperation on graphs and social networks. Nature 441 (7092), 502–505. http://dx.doi.org/10.1038/nature04605
27. Ohtsuki, H., Nowak, M. A., November 2006. The replicator equation on graphs. Journal of Theoretical Biology 243 (7), 86–97. http://dx.doi.org/10.1016/j.jtbi.2006.06.004
28. Ohtsukia, H., Nowak, M., 2008. Evolutionary stability on graphs. Journal of Theoretical Biology 251, 698–707.
29. Rychtar, J., Stadler, B., Winter 2008. Evolutionary dynamics on small-world networks. International Journal of Computational and Mathematical Sciences 2 (1).
30. Santos, F. C., Pacheco, J. M., Lenaerts, T., February 2006. Evolutionary dynamics of social dilemmas in structured heterogeneous populations. PNAS 103 (9), 3490–3494. http://dx.doi.org/10.1073/pnas.0508201103
31. Shakarian, P., Roos, P., 2011. Fast and deterministic computation of fixation probability in evolutionary graphs. In: CIB '11: The Sixth IASTED Conference on Computational Intelligence and Bioinformatics (accepted). IASTED.
32. Slatkin, M., May 1981. Fixation probabilities and fixation times in a subdivided population. Evolution 35 (3), 477–488.
33. Sood, V., Antal, T., Redner, S., 2008. Voter models on heterogeneous networks. Physical Review E (Statistical, Nonlinear, and Soft Matter Physics) 77 (4), 041121. http://link.aps.org/abstract/PRE/v77/e041121
34. Tarnita, C., Ohtsuki, H., Antal, T., Fu, F., Nowak, M., 2009. Strategy selection in structured populations. Journal of Theoretical Biology 259, 570–581.
35. Toran, J., May 2004. On the hardness of graph isomorphism. SIAM J. Comput. 33, 1093–1108. http://dx.doi.org/10.1137/S009753970241096X
36. Van Baalen, M., 2000. Pair approximation for different spatial geometries. In: The geometry of ecological interactions: simplifying spatial complexity. Cambridge University Press, p. 359387.
37. Voelkl, B., Kasper, C., 2009. Social structure of primate interaction networks facilitates the emergence of cooperation. Biology Letters 5, 462–464.
38. Zhou, A.-n., 2011. Stability analysis for various business forms. In: Zhou, Q. (Ed.), Applied Economics, Business and Development. Vol. 208 of Communications in Computer and Information Science. Springer Berlin Heidelberg, pp. 1–7.

Chapter 7
Examining Diffusion in the Real World

7.1 Introduction

In the previous chapters, we introduced various diffusion models and associated "influence maximization" or "seed set" problems. The intuition is that once the problem is solved—a seed set identified—that an information cascade initiating in that set will become wide-spread. However, to date, fitting models such as linear threshold or independent cascade to data has proved difficult—see [1, 2] for examples. Hence, recent data-driven studies have focused on simply detecting if a given cascade will grow in size [3, 5, 7, 10, 11]. In this chapter, we review some of the main results for this "cascade prediction" problem.

It turns out that the cascade prediction problem is difficult due to the frequency of large cascades. Figure 7.1 shows the relationship between cascade size and frequency for retweet traces in a Sina Weibo dataset [4]. This implies that vast major of original contents would only attract little attention from the sociality while only a quite small portion of them can finally become "viral". In this chapter, we differentiate "viral" cascades from "non-viral" ones by the number of reposts as [11] did. In some research, keywords extracted from content or hashtags are also considered as identifiers of a cascade [5]. In addition, researchers may also treat the number of views of a message in social media as its popularity [6]. However, viewing is often considered as a neutral action, viewers may either agree or disagree with the content of a microblog.

Work such as [7] and [9] aimed to discover correlation between centrality measures (such as those described in Chap. 2) of users and their influence in real-world social networks. However, experiments in [7] show that historical influence is a better predictor of actual influence than out degree, furthermore, the combination of them does not work well in terms of predicting actual influence for individual cascade. The authors of [9] claim that shell number of a node is a good predictor of its influence. The correlation between average actual influence and the top fraction of the node in terms of shell number. However, experiments shown in this chapter

© The Author(s) 2015
P. Shakarian et al., *Diffusion in Social Networks*, SpringerBriefs
in Computer Science, DOI 10.1007/978-3-319-23105-1_7

Fig. 7.1 Power-law
distribution of cascade size in
a real-world social network:
2.2 million original
microblogs published in
August, 2011 in Sina Weibo
were monitored until the end
of the month

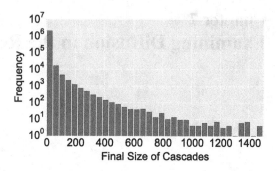

demonstrate low precision for shell number in terms of predicting cascades. Hence, nodal measures, even with other features like historical influence of the root node, are not enough to provide reliable prediction result on cascade size.

Therefore, features extracted from cascades in premature stage (beyond a single node, but only after a small number of individuals have adopted) have been studied to solve this problem [10, 11]. Inspired by "structural diversity" introduced by Ugander et al. [12], the work of Weng et al. [5] extracted features based on distribution of nodes over communities to predict final size of cascades. Recently, in [3] this has been extended to enable *order-of-magnitude* prediction—identification of cascades that will grow ten-fold. We review some of these findings in this chapter.

7.2 Identifying Viral Diffusion Processes: Centrality-Based Approaches

Following along the ideas introduced in Chap. 2 for the SIR model, it would seem sensible to predict how a trend spreads by only examining the root node. In that chapter, nodal measures like degree, pagerank, shell number were used to estimate the influence of a node. However, in real-world social networks, although centrality measures can show some predictability of influence of a node when it seeds cascades, the reliability of this method is shown to be poor.

With data crawled from Twitter, Bakshy et al. [7] trained a regression tree with two group of features of the root nodes shown in Table 7.1. The importance of features are measured by information gain they provides during the splitting process while training the regression tree. In terms of influence of a node, it intuitively represents the size of cascades seeded by it. In that work, historical influence that made by a node is measured by "influence score". The contributors would be assigned a unit influence score (1.0) in total for each repost behavior. In that work, contributors are the active in-coming neighbors who reposted the message before the specific repost published. Three ways they used to assign the influence are: assign the unit influence to the first active in-coming neighbor, assign the unit influence to the latest active in-coming neighbor, assign it uniformly to each active

Table 7.1 Features of root node applied to prediction of influence in [7]

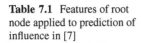

Group 1	Number of followers, number of friends, number of tweets, date of joining
Group 2	Past local influence

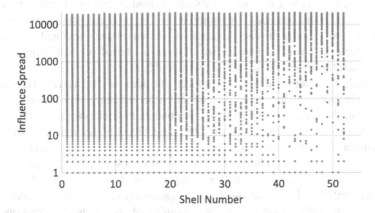

Fig. 7.2 In the Facebook dataset studied by Sen et al. [9], root nodes with the same shell number can result in quite different influence spread value, though it is more effective than other measures

in-coming neighbor ($\frac{1}{N}$). It turns out that these three ways perform quite similarly. The regression tree shows past local influence is the most informative feature while the number of followers (out degree) is the second. Therefore, out degree itself is not informative enough for evaluation of actual influence of the root. This result is consistent with the discovery of another empirical study by Cha et al. [8] on Twitter. Furthermore, their regression result only shows the average predicted influence is approximately linearly correlated to the actual influence with a relatively high standard deviation. This means the prediction actually is quite unreliable for each individual case ($R^2 = 0.34$).

In [9], results of experiment show shell number and two simple heuristics based on it are more effective than in degree and pagerank in terms of measuring the influence of a node in real-world social networks. For evaluation of influence, the authors introduced "influence spread", which is the average number of influenced nodes seeded by roots under all combinations of shell number and in degree value. However, while they showed improvement over the other centrality measures, shell-number alone provides low-precision in predicting viral trends (see Fig. 7.2).

For example, in the Facebook dataset, less than 30 % of the nodes in the top 5 % by shell number are in the set of nodes with top 5 % influence. Moreover, we investigated the influence spread of nodes in the highest shell number. The distribution of historical influence spread for the nodes in the highest shell can be quite varied, for example, 12 % of them have not produced any influence spread at all and 39 % of them only end up with influence spread smaller than half of the maximum. Thus, shell number actually can not provide good precision for identifying nodes that will consistently initiate a large cascade.

7.3   Structural Diversity and Diffusion

As the information provided by the root is not enough to predict the virality of a cascade, then perhaps it is more sensible to instead investigate features based on first N nodes in the cascade. For example, in Cheng et al. [10] the connectivity of the first four nodes in each cascade is shown to be correlated to whether the cascade can reach the median size of cascades based on distribution—hence enabling identification of cascades that will double in size.

In 2012, Ugander et al. [12] introduced the idea of "structural diversity" to explain why some nodes are more susceptible to influence than others. In their experiment, the number of connected components in friendship network crawled from Facebook is applied to measure structural diversity. By structural diversity, they demonstrated that users who received invitations from more various social context are more likely to become a regular Facebook user in their study of the activity of Facebook user recruitment through email. The finding is different from most standard diffusion models—the users potentially infected by this recruitment process are actually not considered as a member of any connected components.[1] This runs counter to the traditional idea that users influenced by more people are more likely to adopt the behavior.

Figure 7.3 shows an example of difference between the size of active neighborhood and structural diversity. In some cases, the size of active in-coming neighborhood even is negatively correlated with the probability of adoption. While the number of connected components in k-core ($k = 2$), k-brace ($k = 2$) or with size larger than $k = 8$ respectively shows strong positive correlation with the likelihood of adoption.

Figure 7.4 illustrates the effect on the probability of adoption when a node is influenced by a certain number of neighbors and communities. This is based on our analysis of data from the microblog Sina Weibo [4]. Instead of measuring the structural diversity by number of connected components, we investigate the probability for users to repost a microblog under the condition of combinations of number of active in-coming neighbors and number of active communities in their in-coming neighborhood. The communities are detected by Louvain algorithm [13] proposed by Blondel et al. which was also used to identify communities in the analysis presented in Chap. 3.

The probability of adoption increases more obviously with the number of active communities than the number of active nodes. One potential explanation for the phenomenon is that communities influence individuals independently. In other words, the person exposed to the influence of multiple sources in the same community may consider them as one because they fail to exhibit independence.

---

[1]This is excepting recent diffusion models created in the aftermath of the publication of [12] such as [15].

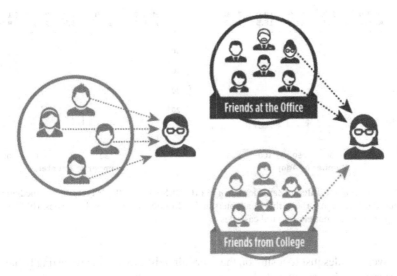

Fig. 7.3 Compared to the right individual, the individual on the *left* has a larger size of active in-coming neighbors while the *right* individual receives stimuli from more communities

Fig. 7.4 Probability of repost for users under different size of in-coming neighborhood and number of in-coming communities, computed using reposting in a 3 month time interval, 5 million users included

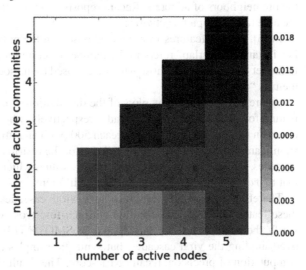

In the recent work of Weng et al. [5], the authors leverage the ideas of structural diversity to accurately identify cascades that will increase by 100 nodes or less. In the recent work of [3], the authors achieve order-of-magnitude prediction, despite the imbalance caused by the power-law distribution of cascade size. In that work, the social network is learned from historical reposts where an edge from user A to user B represents B has reposted at least one microblog from A. Hence, this method can work without any knowledge about the underlying friendship network.

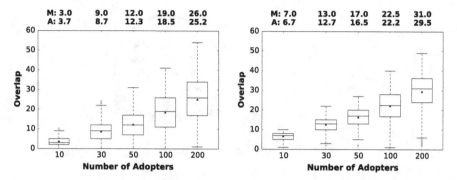

Fig. 7.5 Overlap for different cascade size $m = \{10, 30, 50, 100, 200\}$, 'M' represents median and 'A' represents average. (**a**) Overlap of adopters and λ-frontiers for non-viral cascades. (**b**) Overlap of adopters and λ-frontiers for viral cascades

Moreover, besides just focusing on the users already adopted the reposting behavior (adopters) as other works did, the users exposed to influence of the reposts are also taken into consideration as frontiers. Based on the diffusion network, frontiers are the out neighbors of adopters. Recent reposts from adopters illustrate that frontiers are able to see adopter's activities.

In [3], several features were created based on the notion of structural diversity. For instance, "overlap" refers to the number of common communities represented in the set of adopters and those who are exposed to the social contagion (we refer to them as "frontiers").

Figure 7.5 illustrates box plots of the distribution of a structural diversity based feature for viral and non-viral cascades respectively, where a cascade is viral or not based on whether its final size can reach 500 (with an initial size of 50). Statistically significant difference is shown by KS test for the distribution for the two classes of cascades. KS test outputs extremely small K values which reject the null hypothesis that two distributions are not significantly different.

Therefore, a classifier can recognize viral cascades when is provided with these features. Binary classification with ten-fold cross validation is performed to verify the effectiveness of this approach. SMOTE [14] is also implemented for oversampling the viral cascades, but synthetic samples are not considered during computation of precision, recall or F1 score. The result shown in Fig. 7.6 displays the precision, recall, and F1 for the viral class (2% of samples)—highlighting the effectiveness of these features.

7.4   Conclusion

There are many open problems in the field of information diffusion in social networks. One of the most important topic in the field is about predicting the size of the information cascade and estimate the time when a meme will go viral

Fig. 7.6 Prediction results provided by structural diversity based features extracted from first 50 nodes in cascades. Threshold on final size to distinct viral cascades from non-viral ones is set as 500

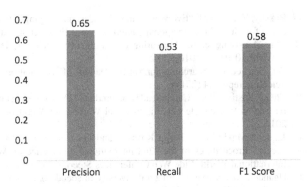

in a social network platform. There are some work trying to learn an influence function from the historic diffusion traces. Work in both areas take advantage of the techniques in machine learning and data mining. There are some preliminary work about sequential seeding to maximize the size of cascades. This is natural extension of the idea. Instead of coming up with all the seeds at the begging and do the expensive simulation for all the time steps, lets come up with a new seed in each time step and let the nature do the computation for us! This is in particular very useful in viral marketing where we can observe the outcome of the diffusion in the real world network.

We also note that almost all the research done in the field uses computer simulation to determine the outcome, and hence resulting in non-realistic observation, or uses past diffusion traces to learn a model. It would also be good to come up with experiments on human subjects to validate our hypotheses.

Finally, there has not been many operational implementation of the systems taking advantage of the ideas proposed in information diffusion in different applications.

References

1. Amit Goyal, Francesco Bonchi, Laks V. S. Lakshmanan, A Data-Based approach to Social Influence Maximization. In PVLDB 2012.
2. Amit Goyal, Francesco Bonchi, Laks V. S. Lakshmanan, Learning Influence Probabilities in Social Networks. In Proc. of the 3rd ACM International Conference on Web Search and Data Mining, WSDM 2010, New York City, 2010.
3. Guo, R., Shaabani, E., Bhatnagar, A., Toward Order-of-Magnitude Viral Cascade Prediction in Social Networks. IEEE/ACM International Conference on Advances in Social Networks Analysis and Mining, 2015.
4. Qian, W., WISE 2012 Challenge 13th International Conference on Web Information Systems Engineering (WISE 2012), 11 May. 2012. Web. 24 May. 2015.
5. Weng, Lilian, Filippo Menczer, and Yong-Yeol Ahn. "Virality prediction and community structure in social networks." Scientific reports 3 (2013).
6. Ma, Haixin, et al. "Towards modeling popularity of microblogs." Frontiers of Computer Science 7.2 (2013): 171–184.

7. Bakshy, Eytan, et al. "Everyone's an influencer: quantifying influence on twitter." Proceedings of the fourth ACM international conference on Web search and data mining. ACM, 2011.
8. Cha, Meeyoung, et al. "Measuring User Influence in Twitter: The Million Follower Fallacy." ICWSM 10.10-17 (2010): 30.
9. Pei, Sen, et al. "Searching for superspreaders of information in real-world social media." Scientific reports 4 (2014).
10. Cheng, Justin, et al. "Can cascades be predicted?" Proceedings of the 23rd international conference on World wide web. International World Wide Web Conferences Steering Committee, 2014.
11. Jenders, Maximilian, Gjergji Kasneci, and Felix Naumann. "Analyzing and predicting viral tweets." Proceedings of the 22nd international conference on World Wide Web companion. International World Wide Web Conferences Steering Committee, 2013.
12. Ugander, Johan, et al. "Structural diversity in social contagion." Proceedings of the National Academy of Sciences (2012): 201116502.
13. Blondel, Vincent D., et al. "Fast unfolding of communities in large networks." Journal of Statistical Mechanics: Theory and Experiment 2008.10 (2008): P10008.
14. Chawla, Nitesh V., et al. "SMOTE: synthetic minority over-sampling technique." Journal of artificial intelligence research 16.1 (2002): 321–357.
15. P. Shakarian, L. Gerdes, H. Lei. Circle-Based Tipping Cascades in Social Networks. WSDM 2014 Workshop on Diffusion Networks and Cascade Analytics (Feb. 2014).

Chapter 8
Conclusion

There are many open problems in the area of diffusion in social networks. First, we believe that data-driven approaches, such as those described in the Chap. 7, are really still in the early stages of development. We have noted that recent work of this type deals with issues such as predicting the influence of individuals nodes, predicting the outcome of a diffusion process, and identifying more realistic models. Work in this area spans from observational studies in disciplines such as sociology and economics to the machine learning approaches seen in the computer science community. As data on real-world diffusion traces become more available, we expect this line of work to grow further.

Sequential seeding is another emerging topic that will likely prove to be important. An individual conducting such marketing operations in practice would likely attempt to adjust ones seeding strategy based on the ongoing dynamics of the process. Though scalability issues seem to loom with this line of work, addressing sequential seeding will likely help better operationalize the ideas described in this volume.

As research on diffusion progresses, we also anticipate to see more human-subjects based tests—which will better validate the approaches and provide fresh insights.

Finally, there are many practical issues concerning the deployment of diffusion ideas in a real-world system. Issues such as collecting and reasoning about social network data in real-time will become paramount. Though challenging, we believe that all of these issues will be addressed as the field progresses—allowing us to harness the power of diffusion in social networks.

© The Author(s) 2015
P. Shakarian et al., *Diffusion in Social Networks*, SpringerBriefs
in Computer Science, DOI 10.1007/978-3-319-23105-1_8

Printed in the United States
By Bookmasters